The LORD Struck the Child

# The LORD Struck the Child

## THE MOST CHILLING PHRASE IN THE BIBLE LEADS US TO HOPE & FREEDOM

by Jeff Smoak

*The Lord Struck the Child*

Copyright © 2011 by Jeff Smoak

Cover Design by Jeff Smoak – image of infant footprint was Macayla's.

Unless otherwise noted, Scripture quotations are taken from the NEW AMERICAN STANDARD BIBLE® Copyright © 1960, 1962, 1963, 1968, 1971, 1972, 1973, 1975, 1977, 1995, by the Lockman Foundation. Used by permission.

ESV refers to the Holy Bible, English Standard Version ® (ESV), copyright © 2001 by Crossway. Used by permission. All rights reserved.

All of the author's royalties of this book will be used to promote the spread of the Gospel, God's glory, and support orphans.

All rights reserved. No part of this book may be reproduced or transmitted in any form or by any means, electronic or mechanical, including photocopying and recording, or by any information storage and retrieval system, without permission from the publisher except as provided by USA copyright law.

ISBN: 978-1-4583-8938-1

Published through Lulu.com, Raleigh, NC

Printed in the United States of America
2011

For Jennifer, Macayla & Jacob and the journey we have been on.

# CONTENTS

**Introduction** — 9
    The Scripture That Rocked My World

**1: What Lies Beneath the Surface?** — 14
    Macayla's Story

**2: The Lord Struck the Child** — 35
    The Story of a Nameless Child

**3: Mourners Strike Back** — 58
    The Story of a Grieving Parent

**4: What is Truth?** — 71
    The Story of a Special-Needs Family

**5: In The Hands of God** — 83
    The Story of Job

**6: In The Hands of Humans** — 97
    The Story of Job's Comfort

**7: The Child Overcomes** — 108
    The Story of a Father and Son

**8: The Lord Saved the Child** — 122
    The Story of Macayla's Healing

**9: Signs** — 141
    The Story of a Community

**10: Become Like a Child** — 156
    The Story of Jacob

**11: New Hope** — 174
    The Story of Our Grief

**Acknowledgments** — 181

**Notes** — 184

# Introduction

## The Scripture that Rocked My World

They say weather can transform our attitude, but not even the beauty of that sunny, spring day could improve my bearing. I was running a few errands in the van and half-listening to the radio. Our full-sized conversion van had a handicap tag hanging from the rearview mirror. In that mirror, I could see the wheelchair lift at the back of the van. It was for our daughter. Three years earlier she had been diagnosed with Battens disease, a rare and fatal brain disorder. It is a genetic disease that has no cure or treatment. In three years, she went from walking, talking and eating to total immobility, tube feedings, blindness and muteness. Soon she would be vegetative and then death would come. Overall, our faith in God had helped us as a family to accept and prepare for this prognosis. But on this particular day, I wasn't doing well. The radio DJ grabbed my full attention when she made a request of her listeners, a request that fueled the storm in me.

The DJ asked listeners to call and share which Scriptures really "rocked" their world. Several people shared warm and fuzzy verses like John 10:10, "I came that they may have life and have it abundantly." Scripture like Jeremiah 29:11 where God says, "For I know the plans that I have for you, plans for welfare and not calamity to give you a future and a hope." These Scriptures really "rocked" some people's worlds, but the Scripture that was making my world "rocky" was 2 Samuel 12:15 "…Then the LORD struck the child…"

This verse had been stuck in my mind for weeks and stirred up questions I thought I had settled; questions I had found peace about earlier. I asked God, "Why?" when our daughter was diagnosed and struggled with that question for over a year. Slowly God's peace overtook the question, though he never fully answered it. But this verse in 2 Samuel ripped off that bandage of peace, revealing the question like an open wound. "The LORD struck the child." Why would God ever strike a child? How can God be good if he does such things? This phrase comes from the story of David and Bathsheba and refers to the child produced by their illicit affair. David, the king of Israel, had Bathsheba's husband killed as part of his plot to cover up the affair. When David confesses his guilt to Nathan the prophet, God takes David's sin away so he would not die, but God declared the child from the affair would die. David's sins were punishable by death under God's Law, but David was spared and this child was "struck" instead. I don't think the radio DJ would have appreciated me calling in and "rocking" her radio show with this verse.

But I was struggling to wrap my mind around the very concept of a loving God who would purposefully strike a child. It was more than just an academic pursuit of theology for me. This was a personal pursuit of theology. Had my child been "struck?" Did God strike my child or did she simply have an unfortunate draw of the cards in a fallen world? Being a seminary student, I studied the text and looked it up in commentaries and pulled academic articles. I broke down the Hebrew as best as I could, considering I had not taken any Hebrew courses yet. I read books on God's sovereignty and our suffering, but very few had directly dealt with this verse and when they did it was unsatisfactory. Often the focus was on the "wonderful grace" David received from God and David's repentance, but completely ignored the fact God was killing a child. Others simply portrayed God's action as capricious and cruel, ignoring the input of other portions of Scripture, which describe God as "gracious, merciful, slow to anger and abounding in steadfast love, and relenting from disaster." (Jonah 4:2) How can God be gracious and merciful, sparing an evil city of nonbelievers like Nineveh, but strike the believer's child for the believer's sin? To call this discipline from the heavenly Father seems insane (see Hebrews 12). The radio DJ was trying to be positive and encouraging, but I grew more cynical by the moment. I so much wanted to call in and scream that Scripture's sole purpose was NOT to be a source of warm and fuzzy feelings. Why did so many people want to call in and claim the blessings promised in Scripture and ignore the curses and warnings in Scripture? Why did so many commentators skip over the verses about God striking the child?

What does this mean about God and my life, not only as a believer, but simply as a human on planet earth?

## WHAT THIS BOOK IS AND WHAT IT IS NOT

In the pages to follow, these and more questions are examined through stories of people like David and Bathsheba. We will look at the story of a man named Job and the story of my daughter. We will look at stories of others who have lost their children, one of whom may surprise you. Included are blog entries from our website and private journal, which chronicled Macayla's life after the diagnosis. These entries are not in chronological order, but are placed because of their relationship to the discussion. Maybe, through these pages, we can come to peace about God's sovereignty and our suffering. Maybe we can find hope and encouragement and less cynicism. Maybe we can learn to worship this God in spite of our pain. Maybe, just maybe, by looking at the horrible and hideous circumstances in these stories, we can find liberation in the midst of any situation. Then again, maybe not. This is not a safe subject to tackle.

Maybe you have picked up this book because the title "The Lord Struck the Child" stirred curiosity and you want to see how I will reveal and clarify that God never *really* struck a child. Here's the rub. God did strike the child and it cannot be explained away; studied and understood better, but not explained away. Maybe you are desperately searching for a way to reconcile your stated beliefs with the horror of losing a child of your own. Whatever has brought you to these pages, know that this book is not a theological treatise on a good God and the existence of evil, though some of this issue will be tackled. It is not solely a memoir of our family's painful struggle, though you will know much of it by the end. This book is intended to convey the perspective and hope we found on our journey. The book is a journey itself, sharing some of God's wonderful promises, even from some of the most troubling portions of Scripture. This book is intended to encourage discipleship and growth. This book shares Macayla's story to bring perspective to those who are navigating the blessings and struggles of daily life, and to encourage those who are in very dark places. This book is meant to help you walk through any circumstance, the good, the bad, and the ugly, with a renewed sense of God's grace, truth and presence. This book is intended to help you discover your true identity.

Unfortunately, we so often let our circumstances define us. We start thinking of ourselves as victims in tough times and can even consider ourselves to be failures. In prosperous times, we can think too much of ourselves and attribute our fortune to our own luck or prowess, taking God for granted. On this journey, we can discover there is an identity offered to us that is stable, eternal and not governed by the whims of circumstances. As we ask tough questions about God in tough circumstances, we must ask tough questions about ourselves. Each chapter includes such questions and honestly answering these can be steps for growth. I encourage you to ponder and pray over these questions and write down your answers as you go. The most important question you must answer on this journey is, "Are you a child of God?" Many think that all humans are children of God, but this is not true. We are all creations of God, but not all are his children. Jesus was very clear on this point and it is recorded for us in John 8:31-47. "Am I a child of God?" This question must echo repeatedly on this journey. Its answer will determine all the other answers we seek.

I have heard some preachers say we will never know why God "allows" or "causes" certain things to happen so we only need to ask the question, "What?" As in, "What does God want me to learn and do in the midst of my situation?" This is a good question, but never asking "Why?" is not as sage as some may think. Throughout the Bible, God's people faithfully and legitimately ask "why" when faced with tragedy. Certainly, asking "what" is a healthy and faithful question. But the heart still longs for "why." The intellect still searches for "why." To ignore "why" is to deprive our hearts and minds of an important, if not crucial, step to draw closer to God. The Psalmists and prophets asked God "why" and those questions have been preserved for us in God's word. It is the same Word where many answers can be found.

In no way can I tell you God will give you a complete answer to your "Why?" On the other hand, he may indeed. He is God after all. But asking this question can lead us to other questions that certainly need answering. "Why?" leads us to, "Who is God?" and "What is the world really like?" and "How and where do I fit into this world?" and "What is the point of my life, the blessings and the struggles?" and "Is God's word really sufficient to guide me through life?" I believe the answer to this last question is, "Yes!" God says his word is a lamp unto our feet (Ps. 119:105). A lamp illuminates just enough of the path ahead for the next step, not the next ten miles. But for us to see the light and take that next step, we cannot be blind. We have to open our eyes, our minds, and our hearts on this journey. Make no mistake; this journey is not safe. It will take us through the valley of the shadow of death. The answers to these questions will define our lives and impact everyone with whom we come into contact. "Why?" leads us to the question, "Am I a child of God?" God adopts us as his children when we receive what Christ (the begotten Child) did for us at the cross. But this question, as well as its follow-up question, must be answered. "What does it mean to be a child of God?" I think Russell Moore's comments about adoption also apply here:

> But adoption is contested, both in its cosmic and missional aspects. The Scriptures tell us there are unseen beings in the air around us who would rather we not think about what it means to be who we are in Christ. These rulers of this age would rather we ignore both the eternal reality and the earthly icon of it. They would rather we find our identity, our inheritance, and our mission according to what we can see and verify as ours – according to what the Bible calls "the flesh" – rather than according to the veiled rhythms of the Spirit of life. That is why adoption isn't charity – it's war.[1]

Has God adopted you? We must seek our answers and identity in Spirit and Truth, or we will lose our way on this journey. We will lose the war for our identity. Am I a child of God or a child of circumstances and whims?

# 1
# What Lies Beneath the Surface?
## *Macayla's Story*

"Enough!" One December evening in 2004, my wife and I came to this conclusion. We both were working fulltime while our two children went to daycare. I was attending seminary part-time. We were over committed and stressed out. We came to the conclusion we needed to fully submit to the call of ministry and move to seminary fulltime. We began researching and praying to determine if we should continue at the seminary where I had started or go elsewhere. We put our house on the market. We would either move closer to our current seminary or to any seminary God directed us. Two months later, February 2005, our prayers and research were answered as God made it abundantly clear we were to move to New Orleans Baptist Theological Seminary. Our house sold in March and was scheduled to close in April. Our circumstances were flowing along as predicted and God was opening and shutting all the "right" doors.

But in late March, our daughter, Macayla, began to have some strange episodes. She seemed to fall occasionally without warning, but we could never actually witness a whole event to discover the cause. She was almost four years old at the time and she would not or could not tell us what was happening. On a Friday morning, about two weeks into these "episodes", I saw her have one while she put a puzzle together. She was sitting on her knees in the floor and leaning over the puzzle when she suddenly paused. He torso bounced with slight convulsions and her arms went limp. She began to fall face-first toward the floor but she stopped herself just in time and went back to putting the puzzle together as if nothing happened. The whole event took two or three seconds. My wife,

Jennifer, is a nurse and thought it could be a seizure. In response, our pediatrician lined up a CT scan and some tests for the following Monday.

Tuesday evening after the tests, Macayla started running a fever and having more episodes. Her fever lasted into the next morning and she collapsed multiple times without warning. She bloodied her lips, bruised her face and was visibly frightened. The doctor admitted her to the hospital where they ran multiple tests for the next three days. Her blood work, spinal fluid, and MRI were all labeled as normal. The only medical problems Macayla had prior to this was a mild speech delay and kidney reflux, but nothing that seemed to be related to these episodes. While we were in the hospital, we worked in a routine follow-up for the kidney reflux. They did a renal ultrasound to view her kidneys and inadvertently discovered she had gallstones! This won her a surgery a little over a month later. This was not related, but just seemed to be pain on top of pain.

At this point, we were not asking, "Why?" We were mainly asking, "What?" What was wrong with our daughter? What should we do for her? What was happening to her? In the meantime, we were about to close on the sale of our home and move into a rental house for a couple of months. We were still going through the process of being accepted into the masters program in New Orleans. We were working, paying bills, going to church, doctor visits and so on. But through all of these things, we had not really asked why God would allow this to happen to Macayla after telling us to go to New Orleans. We were just dealing with what was in front of us at the moment. Calamity can keep us too busy to ask God, "Why?"

Macayla's episodes became more frequent over the next month and after twenty-four hours on an EEG, it was confirmed she was having over one hundred seizures per day. Most of these were not noticeable from the outside. From her perspective, she was losing blocks of time, each lasting three to ten seconds, and she was loosing over 100 blocks per day. The seizures visible to us involved her falling, going limp in her arms or myoclonic jerks. We started her on medication and over the next two months we ran a battery of tests our geneticists called "The Million-Dollar Work-up," but the cause of the epilepsy remained unknown. This is when we began to question if we should still move to New Orleans, but when the doctors could not discover the culprit for the seizures, we decided to move forward. God told us to go there and surely he was not surprised by Macayla's seizures even if we were. At no point during our prayer times or Bible study did we find God pulling back the reins on the plan to move. Besides, there was a children's hospital in New Orleans with an epilepsy center. We thought it might be the best place for Macayla. So, we quit our jobs and moved from Greenville, South Carolina to New Orleans in August 2005.

It was the most efficient and successful move we ever made. We were unpacked and set up within four days and I started classes. God provided the funds we needed through family, friends and the sale of our home. Jennifer found a job as a public-school nurse and was set to start in a couple of weeks. As I did course work, Jennifer began looking for childcare options and exploring pediatricians. But two weeks after we moved in, we were evacuating New Orleans in front of hurricane Katrina. We still were not asking, "Why?" yet, but we were asking, "What?" and "How?" We wondered how long we would be evacuated. We wondered what to do next. But "why" came shortly thereafter once we discovered the full extent of the damage. The levees around New Orleans broke and flooded the city. It would be at least a year before we could go back. Why would God plainly lead us to go to New Orleans when he knew hurricane Katrina was coming? Why would he let this happen when we were being obedient to him? Why would God allow this as our daughter struggled with epilepsy, gallstones, speech delays and developmental delays?

I heard multiple preachers proclaim the hurricane was God's judgment on New Orleans, the modern-day Sodom and Gomorrah. Such statements angered me, as we knew there were plenty of godly people in New Orleans serving God's kingdom. Was God judging these folks too? Was he judging and punishing us in the midst of our obedience to him? Besides, I thought God's punishment was poured out at the cross, not in a hurricane. But still, we are dealing with a sovereign God who "is in control." Why did he let this happen? Did he cause it or just permit it? Suffering and pain have long been the skeptic's ammunition for firing on the existence of a good and loving God. It seemed hurricane Katrina brought out droves of skeptics on one end and divine-retribution preachers on the other while we were in the middle asking, "Why?" Neither the skeptics nor the preachers of smite had much to offer.

We also had certain family and friends look at our situation and declare they knew God's will for us. Before we moved, we were told Macayla's seizures were a sign from God for us not to go to New Orleans. Those who thought this never seemed to carry their logic to its conclusion. They were essentially saying God struck our child with epilepsy to keep us from moving. Of course, once we moved and the hurricane came, this was another "sign" from God we were not meant to be in New Orleans. Again, the logical conclusion is that God orchestrated a deadly hurricane, killed over one thousand people, just to communicate with the Smoak family. I found it interesting how these were signs, yet it was not a sign that all of our needs were met to go to seminary by means beyond our own capacity. Needless to say, those who appealed to the idea God communicates through circumstances more than Scripture, prayer and worship were not very helpful. We were asking God questions only he could answer.

In the midst of our evacuation, God did not answer the question about "why" but he did answer "how" and "what." Through family, church, and friends, we were provided a house, clothing, food, furniture, funds, and even toys for the kids. There was so much abundance that we were able to pass on quite a bit to other evacuated families. I was able to continue my course work on the Internet. We evacuated to Anderson, South Carolina, which was close enough to Greenville that Jennifer was able to return to the hospital for work. Macayla and our son, Jacob, enjoyed their "new" used toys immensely and adjusted quite well to their new surroundings. Macayla's seizures had taken their toll and she was digressing developmentally. Her walking resembled that of an advanced toddler and she labored to run. But she loved to explore. The house we were in was in a rural setting and she loved to walk as far as I would let her. We often walked through a small field adjacent to the house. She would pause and drop to her knees in the grass to feel the textures and pick up dry leaves. She would halfway listen to my commands to not go too far. I was on the constant lookout for fire-ant beds, as she was unable to fully understand the danger at that point. For her the world was full of wonder and new things. She worried over little, or at least it seemed that way. As long as she could explore her surroundings and there was cheese in the refrigerator, she was good to go.

Unfortunately, Macayla's medications were not keeping pace with the seizures. Her speech was no longer just a delay, but a disorder. Her words and sounds became labored while new sounds she previously could not make suddenly came out. She knew the word "mine" but it started coming out as "mice." By Thanksgiving 2005, Macayla stopped running and only walked. She had more falling spells and injuries. In December we did a follow-up MRI to compare to the one we had in April. There were definite changes in Macayla's brain. She had increased deterioration in the cerebellum, which on an MRI looks like a head of cauliflower at the base of the brain. It controls motor functions. There was also deterioration throughout the rest of the brain that had not been present on the previous scan. Our neurologist told us the MRI's and increased developmental digression narrowed down our search for an answer. He suggested some specific tests to discover which degenerative disease could be causing the brain damage. Two days after Christmas, our neurologist gave us the news. It was Battens disease.

"Why?" The diagnosis of Battens disease and its deadly prognosis for our daughter brought everything to a halt. All of the struggles over the past year had kept us so busy we did not take time to ponder the question "Why?" But now it was the only question we asked. It was my main focus. Why did God allow this rare disease to strike our child? I carried a mutated gene that combined with a mutated gene in my wife to produce this horrible disease in our daughter. Macayla had been a healthy child and intelligent. She was quiet but she had a great sense of humor. She showed no real problems with the exception of the mild speech delay around age two. It took eight months after the first seizures to come to a diagnosis (we were fortunate it didn't take longer). As soon as Jennifer and I got the news, we sat in the doctor's parking lot crying and praying. Why us? Why Macayla? We wanted to circle the wagons and keep everyone out. We wanted to just hold Macayla and her brother, Jacob. He was two years younger than her. Did he have it too? We were scared, devastated, and not sure what to do next.

We were being obedient to God and going into ministry as a family. I had struggled with the decision to go to New Orleans in the first place because it is such a dangerous city. I was concerned I would not be able to protect Jennifer and the kids in such a crime-ridden place. But, with the wisdom and encouragement of my wife, I gave in to be obedient to God. As it turned out, crime and violence did not strike us but a hurricane and mutated genes did. I couldn't protect my daughter from this horrible disease. The prognosis was fatal and there was no cure or treatments. What was God thinking? How could he let this happen to us?

Outside the City: blog for August 16, 2006

Macayla is playing on the floor and looking through a book about Jonah. Jonah the prophet of God who was sent to the city of Nineveh to deliver God's message... To my surprise, God made it abundantly clear that we were to go to New Orleans for seminary. My biggest hang up with New Orleans was the crime rate. How could I protect my family in a city where the murder rate was ten times the national average? I feared that such a decision was putting my family in danger, but Jenny reminded me that ultimately I could only protect her and the children so much because, in short, I'm not God...

Jonah was a prophet who was told to go to a violent city he didn't want to go to. After some rebellion and prayer, he finally went and did what God commanded. But Jonah (on one level) had expected God to act after the message was delivered. The message was, "Forty days and Nineveh will fall." It was NOT "Nineveh will fall unless you repent." No, Nineveh was supposed to fall. So Jonah delivered the message and sat outside the city to watch the fireworks. But the fireworks never came because Nineveh repented. God had not acted like Jonah expected. Jonah was angry, so angry he wanted to die. I did what God wanted. I went to a wicked city after rebellion and prayer, but God has not acted as I would have expected. (Of course, I wasn't going to deliver a message of judgment, but to go and learn to share a message of hope.)[ii] So here I am. Outside the city wondering what God is up to. But I spoke to a man who recently lost his little, infant girl suddenly. She died in her crib. Listening to him and his story made me realize that I stay too focused on what I think God should be doing. Instead, maybe I should be focused on what God is ACTUALLY doing.

## QUESTION THE QUESTIONER

Catastrophe raises the basic question of "why?" but before we get to the content of the question and some possible answers, we must draw out the intent of the questioner. With what spirit are we asking? Are we asking, "Why?" in rhetorical cynicism or do we really want an answer? I believe, even in our most cynical and angry moment, we still want an answer in our innermost being. However, why do we fail to ask the same question when faced with good fortune? If we did ask, would we ask rhetorically or really look for the answer? That is not a rhetorical question, by the way. When horrible circumstances strike our lives, we can be quick to shake our fists at God and ask, "Why?" But when fortunate circumstances come into our lives, we chalk it up to luck, our own prowess, or believe we deserve it. If we actually credit God for our blessings, then do we really ask why he gave them to us?

Most of the time we assume a good God is supposed to heap blessings on us and make things go our way because he loves us. God becomes a divine lottery of sorts. Many health and wealth preachers, especially those on television, chalk life's blessings up to God rewarding their faith. For them, blessings are a reflection of how faithful they are and how their "faith" compels God to reward them. They reduce God to a divine vending machine. Just drop in a few quarters of faith, and he will spit out a candy bar of blessing for you! But if we ask God why he has blessed us in a certain way, we might discover he wants us to use those blessings for his kingdom and not our own. Let's be honest and admit we are not too keen on that idea.

# THREE LEVELS OF CAUSE AND EFFECT IN MY DIET

We struggle with the question for another reason. Our perspective can be very limited, especially at times of extreme fortune or catastrophe. We tend to be pragmatic thinkers always looking for the cause and effect of circumstances but not the cause and effect within our hearts and minds. In other words, we often only look at the surface.

After evacuating New Orleans, my wife was working and I was doing course work. It was a natural fit for me to stay at home with Macayla. She was not old enough for school and the daycares were not equipped for her needs. I noticed something strange begin to happen shortly thereafter. My clothes began to shrink and then expand again. I noticed it especially in the waist of my pants as I tried to button them. My weight began to fluctuate but mostly it went higher and higher. I began to realize that in spite of the busy schedule Macayla's care created, I was not being active enough or exercising. Simple enough. Lack of physical activity leads to weight gain. I just needed to carve out some time to exercise and all would be well, right? But someone had to care for Macayla while I worked out and at first that was not possible. So, for a while I had to suck in the gut while buttoning the pants. But it was not long before Macayla had a wheelchair and I could push her as I walked. When she reached the age to go to a special-needs class in public school, I was able to work out on a consistent basis. Thus, I lost weight. I worked out consistently for a year and a half. I heard people say that if you do something for sixty days, it will become a life-long habit. Not true! I was consistent for a year and a half in my exercise, but was able to literally stop that habit overnight! I cannot even remember what made me stop going, but I stopped and my clothes began to shrink again. When I exercised, I lost weight. When I didn't exercise, I put on weight. Simple cause and effect.

However, there was more going on than caloric intake and output. We must dig deeper to expose why we react to the circumstances in our lives the way we do. This goes to the cause and effect on a deeper level and these are links in the chain we usually ignore. Was my weight gain simply because of a schedule that made exercise impossible or was there something else at work? Our situation was stressful, emotional and difficult to fathom.

Could it be that food increasingly became a source of comfort and a coping mechanism? It was easy to miss this because as soon as my "circumstances allowed" me to have a regular exercise time, I got busy and lost weight. It was the first time I wore size 34 jeans since college! How, in spite of this success, was I able to so easily quit exercising after doing it consistently for eighteen months? Maybe the exercise simply replaced the food as a source of comfort. Maybe both the exercise and food were coping mechanisms trying to fill a void only Christ could.

This brings up the question, "Do I really know and trust that the Holy Spirit is my Comforter?" To discover and analyze what motivates our decisions and reactions, we must go below the surface, deeper than the circumstantial level. The deeper, motivational level is where we find what desires and values are driving our decisions in the midst of our circumstances. It is where we find our emotions and worldview. It is where we see if our intellect or emotion is driving our decisions. It is where our past experience motivates and influences our current decisions.

Then we can go to a deeper level, into the cause and effects on the greater plain of reality. This involves reality beyond our motivations. I could ask, "Why does God care if I gain weight? How does my body mass or eating habits impact my relationship with God? Why did God let me get into this situation in the first place? Why did my daughter have Battens disease? Isn't it God's fault I am a sedentary, stay-at-home father?" We so often want to ask these deepest, cosmic level questions but only expect circumstantial answers. We expect those answers to come in the form of solutions to our problems. For nonbelievers, these questions obviously do not involve God. For them, there is no God directing events here on earth. They can ask, "Why?" but for them the answers lie in statistics and probability. They simply have to cope and there are a plethora of coping options to choose. For believers, there are answers. But many believers hope that by challenging God on the reasons for our situation, he will somehow make our circumstances more to our liking.

But what if we got an answer? What if God answered our question but our circumstances did not change? If God told us the greater, cosmic reason our child died but it did not change the fact that our child was dead, would we be satisfied? If God told us the greater cosmic, reason our job was lost but we were still unemployed, would we be satisfied? I often get so wrapped up in my circumstances I can barely see past them. In fact, I believe God often gives me answers but I am so deafened by my situation I do not hear. Unfortunately, if we hear the answers, we may not be satisfied because God's reasons are not ours. In other words, his reasons may not sound good enough to us.

Many believers cope with bad circumstances the same way nonbelievers do because they do not want to truly dig deeper and cannot hear God's answers. It is easier to cope by getting lost in entertainment, alcohol, drugs, sexual gratification, or a plate of our favorite food than to truly look below the surface. I certainly did not want to go before God with my idols, be it comfort food or exercise endorphins, because I would have to face up to my shame and lack of trust. I would have to face the reality that I have tried to use food or activity to fill a void only God was meant to fill. I would much rather eat hot-glazed doughnuts and have God miraculously keep me thin, but he doesn't seem interested in my diet plan. Thus, honestly, it is much easier to do what feels good than to do what is good. It seems my motivations are not in sync with the cosmic cause and effect of God's plan.

## WHO'S IN CHARGE AROUND HERE?

Sovereignty is another factor driving the question of why we suffer. Tragedies show us very quickly we are not in control of our lives. We may get quite angry when we discover the control we thought we had was merely an illusion and even a delusion. What do we truly control? Even the remote control for our television only obeys our wishes if it has batteries, is not broken and the television it communicates with is operational. Multiple factors beyond our control within a television set can cause it to not function. Don't get me started on computers! These are simple matters. What of life's weightier matters? We cannot completely control our health. We cannot control the other drivers on the road who could collide with us. We cannot control natural disasters. We cannot control many diseases. At best we can only hope to influence these things, but we are never sovereign over them.

When we ask, "Why?" we are taking a first step toward

realizing the minimal control we have over our own lives. There would be no reason to ask the question if we were the ones who were sovereign. Anger and frustration are reflections of this realization. As I write these words, my son is angry over a video game that is not working as he expects. His attitude reminds me of his father when he plays video games. Anger was also common emotion for me throughout our daughter's disease. I was so angry because I could not help her and God would not heal her. Anger and "Why?" are natural responses to tragedy and can be positive steps, if through them we realize sovereignty over life was never ours to be had.

It would be impossible in a world like ours for any of us to be truly sovereign over our lives. We would have to be in complete control of every person with whom we come into contact as well as the people who influence them. We would have to possess complete control over disease, weather, media, electronics, machines, the power company, the phone company, etc. All of these things impact our lives in various degrees and we would have to be completely sovereign over them to be truly sovereign over our life. Even if we moved to a desert island away from people and off the grid, we would still have to be sovereign over the weather, tides, disease, food sources and water. But since there are six billion people on the planet, there is no possible way for each of us to be equally and fully sovereign over our own lives. Certainly we all have the ability to make choices, but our choices are not the only ones being made. The choices of others also impact us. In a universe like ours, either no one is sovereign or only one person can be sovereign. In other words, if there is a sovereign God, then we cannot be in control. If there is no God, then we still cannot be in control. No matter what, we are not in control. I honestly do not like this fact many days.

There is another reason we struggle with the concept of God's sovereignty. We know we "freely" make choices. So, how can God be in control while we make free choices? Here again, we do not live in a vacuum. What influences our choices? Do we really make "free" choices? Think of all the outward influences that impact our decisions. But do not stop there because we must also consider the motivational influences below the surface. Human nature and flaws impact our decisions. Our past, present and future plans influence our choices as well. Our decision-making process is impacted to various degrees by hundreds, if not thousands, of influences and we are usually only aware of one or two at best. Exactly how freely do we make decisions? This is not to say we are programmed robots. We make choices, but an infinite and all-powerful God knows how we are influenced to make decisions. Only he could know how every nuance of our life, from our health to the funny look that person gave us in traffic, plays into our decisions. Thus, he can weave our choices into a greater plan of his sovereign design. Only a God like this could truly understand how each of us makes choices and how those decisions interact with the actions and choices of others. In a manner that is beyond our current comprehension, God sovereignly weaves everyone's choices into a design. This mystery is a stumbling block for many and a motivator to ask, "Why?" in the midst of tragedy.

## IS GOD JUST RUBBING HIS ALMIGHTINESS IN MY FACE?

This leads us to the basic hurdle we must all overcome. Perspective. Since we are so ensnared by time and space, we import those limitations into our understanding of God and the whole of reality. When I state "the whole of reality," I am speaking of not only the space-time universe, or what most folks call the "real" world, but also the eternal realm of God who is transcendent of time and space. Most people call this the spiritual world. But the whole of reality includes both of these things. Unfortunately, most people consider the spiritual to be less real and the physical to be more real when in fact it is just the opposite. The eternal God of the universe is more real than anything or anyone we experience here on earth since all that is made came from him. Typically, we think of God as transcendent and detached from our "reality" but when a tragedy has come into our life, we stop thinking of God as detached. We are thinking he may have something to do with our lives and we are not too happy about it.

People often view God as egotistical and arbitrary. The Bible tells us we are to worship God and he is perfect, holy and great. Further, we are supposed to believe the Bible was inspired by God and is composed of the words he chose. So the "autobiography" of God is often seen as a difficult-to-understand document containing many of God's "conceited" statements. In the Bible, God is repeatedly demanding that humans worship him. He seems to arbitrarily bless some people in the stories while he curses and kills others. He has rule after rule and people debate as to which rules are important, which ones are symbolic, and which, if any, can be ignored. What are we to make of all this? It is true the Bible is a revelation of God. True Christians declare the Bible is God's word and he inspired it. The Bible is completely true. But this does not mean God is egotistical and arbitrary. Before we can understand this, we must expand our perspective.

## Prayers for More Time: blog for June 3, 2009

Over the course of two weeks, Jacob continued to ask us how much longer Macayla will be with us and we have repeated the answer we gave before as talked about in an earlier post. A couple of mornings ago, Macayla wet her bed so I moved her to the bed with Jennifer so I could change Macayla's sheets. About that time Jacob woke up and for some reason he went straight into Macayla's room. Upon seeing she was not in the bed, he got a worried look on his face and anxiously asked, "Where's Macayla?" He was relieved to discover her snuggling with mom and he joined them. Jacob asked me again yesterday afternoon how long Macayla would live. Later, at bedtime, Jacob said his prayers and thanked God for our family and prayed for Macayla:

"God, thank you for Macayla. Please let her stay with us a long time. Help her live to ten y...Help her stay with us three ye...Lord, keep her with us for five more years."

It reminded me of the story of Abraham "negotiating" with God over Sodom and Gomorrah's fate. I don't believe we ever negotiate with God, but He welcomes our requests like this because we stand to learn through the process. My hope is Jacob and our family learns that God hears our prayers and even if He says no, we will still trust Him. It's hard when God will not do things the way we want, especially if we are asking for something good like extending a life. But our view is limited. Our knowledge is limited. God's is not. But still, we pray Macayla will surprise us as she usually does and be with us longer than predicted. However long she is with us, when it is over we will not have to ask, "Where's Macayla?" We know she is in His hands and He promises that is non-negotiable.

If God is truly all-powerful, all-knowing, good, loving, just, merciful, and the Creator of the universe, then it obviously stands to reason he is not like us. It stands to reason there is a vast, in fact, infinite difference between the only all-powerful Being (by definition there can only be one all-powerful being) and creatures such as us. We are limited in power and ability. We are limited in our knowledge, lifespan, language, and perspective. Obviously we are not devoid of these things, but ours is finite. God, in order for him to truly be God, is infinitely powerful, knowing, seeing, present, existing, and his perspective is infinitely above our own. This is why it is ludicrous for us to say God is conceited or arbitrary. We cannot see or know all that he sees and knows. It is not conceited for God to say he is holy and perfect, because he is in fact holy and perfect. David Platt says it best:

> God is at the center of his universe and everything he does ultimately revolves around him. If this is true, we may wonder, then does this make God selfish? How can God's purpose be to exalt himself? This is a good question, and it causes us to pause until we ask the follow-up question: Whom else would we have him exalt? At the very moment God exalted someone or something else, he would no longer be the great God worthy of all glory in all the universe, which he is.[iii]

When God speaks of his holiness and perfection, it is not to rub it in our faces. It is simply a report on the facts. It is a direct response to the question, "What is God like?" This is the question we ask in the deepest recesses of our souls. "Is God real? What is He like?" The Bible gives us answers to these questions. It gives us the facts that God is holy, perfect and deserves to be worshiped for who he is. It is not inflated flattery, but truth. However, we often do not hear the answers over the blare of our circumstances and egos. God has answered our deepest question of what he is like and sadly we do not believe it because we do not like the answer.

## Plain Fact: blog for November 26, 2007

My four-year-old, Jacob, and I were talking about buying Jennifer a Christmas present and I asked him what he thought his mom would like. He first said that she likes food and we should get her some food. (He also suggested we get this for his eye doctor since "Dr. Tony helps us so much.")

"Mom does like food," I agreed. "What other things does she like?"

"She likes me," Jacob said.

I agreed again and said, "But you already are a gift to us."

In a very matter-of-fact tone he said, "Yes, I am. God sent me and I'm a present and everyone thinks I'm cute."

I laughed a little and he said, "What's so funny?"

Jacob wasn't being conceited when he stated that everyone thinks he's cute. Many times when we are around other people, he often hears them say that he is so cute. From his standpoint, it is just the truth. It is a plain fact that he has learned because so many people around him have reinforced it. What we may mistake for conceit is simply Jacob making a plain and true statement. We may think that God is conceited when He states that He is worthy to be worshiped and praised. We may think it is conceit when God says He should be at the center of our lives. But the fact is that it is true and just like Jacob,

God is not trying to talk it up to make Him feel better about Himself. He is simply sharing the facts and it is therefore not conceit or vanity. Maybe this is why Jesus tells us to become like a child (not childish) so that we can recognize truth and trust it. As Jacob's parent, I can attest that he is pretty darn cute. As an adopted son of God and as a parent that watches God work through Jacob, I can attest that our Father in heaven is worthy to be worshiped and praised. It is plain fact.

## THE LIMITED VIEW FROM MY UNLIMITED EGO CHATEAU

Ironically, our limited perspective makes us, not God, egocentric. When we ask, "Why?" about our situation, we assume it is all about us. After the hurricane and Macayla's diagnosis, I often asked God why he would allow this to happen to *us* in the midst of *our* obedient move to seminary. I wanted to know why a horrible disease struck *my* child. I wanted to know why *my* life was turned upside down. When tragedy comes, typically we only see how it affects *our* lives. But the impact of our circumstances reaches further than we can imagine. Even the smallest decision we make on any given day has impacts that ripple through our family, community and future generations.

Our presence alone impacts people and circumstances in ways we can't begin to inventory. When and where I choose to shop for groceries doesn't just impact the store and its suppliers, but also impacts the day of other people in traffic, in the store, and the person working the checkout. Our decision to actually stop at a traffic light and not race through the intersection when it is yellow may frustrate the person behind us, and it will impact the timeline of their day. They may reach their destination a minute later and run into a person they would have missed otherwise. That interaction could lead to opportunities or problems depending on the relationship. On and on the chain of events could go and our minds get swallowed by the seemingly infinite possible chain reactions. The point is, we rarely think about how far reaching our daily, mundane decisions can be and we especially do not think of it in the midst of tragic circumstances. This is not to say we must sweat every choice. It is simply the observation we are not center of the universe. My family was not the only family to flee New Orleans. My daughter was not the only child affected by Battens disease. Through those tragedies we met people we would never have met otherwise. We have relationships with people as a direct result of these circumstances. We have impacted their lives and they have impacted ours. We moved to a community where we never planned on living. This has impacted the people of that community and us in various ways.

We send ripples out all the time and hardly notice. However, it would be foolish to consider any of these outcomes as "the reason" God allowed the hurricane and Battens. What I am describing are simply circumstantial results of our situation. These are links in the chain of events. We are not capable of knowing all of the results that will ripple out of a situation like ours. We will never know how many people our tragedy has impacted and in turn how many people they have impacted. Circumstantial results are not the same thing as the "reason" for our situation, but they certainly can correlate to the reason. Obviously, God utilizes the chain of events in our life to impact the chain of events in other people's life and vice versa. We will delve deeper into cosmic-level reasons later. For now, we must admit our perspective is limited and egocentric. In our pride, we try to make ourselves the center of the universe, building a perspective that is aloof to others and the world around us. We attempt to become self-sufficient bourgeois living in the Chateau de Egotism. But our perspective expands and gains clarity when we see past ourselves and realize our lives have broad impact and are part of a bigger plan. This plan, by the way, is not ours.

## THE SHAPE OF OUR INTENTIONS

When we ask why a good God would allow our suffering, we need to be aware of our intent behind the question. Our intentions are shaped by our perspective and worldview. Is our question about God rhetorical and asked in antagonizing skepticism? Even if it is, the questioner, in his heart of hearts, wants an answer. However, if a confused believer asks the question, what is shaping it? The questioner must be aware of the theology shaping their intentions. People often shun the word theology as academic and impractical, but there is nothing more practical. Theology is simply the study of God. The ramifications of God's existence and character affect every human that has or ever will live on the planet. The ramifications are of great importance to our morality, daily choices, our purpose for existence, and our eternal state. Everyone on the planet has a theological stance.

Atheism is as much of a theological position as Christianity. It takes faith to believe there is no God since there is no empirical proof concerning his existence one way or the other. Of course, both atheists and believers claim there is a plethora of evidence for their position, but notice we are talking about proof, not merely evidence. It is not wishful thinking to believe God exists when it has not been empirically proven one way or another. An atheist could have as much psychological need for God to not exist as a theist could have for God to exist. It would only be wishful thinking if it were a belief held in spite of opposing, empirical proof.[iv] Before we ask God why, we indeed may need to ask ourselves, "What?" What do we believe about God? If we believe God exists, then what is he like? What can I know about him? Of course it helps to explore these questions before tragedy comes because in the midst of loss and anguish, the emotions are raw and explosive. The intellect is numb and analyzing presuppositions becomes impossible. Unfortunately, most of us wait until tragedy strikes before we ask any questions at all. In the midst of blessing and prosperity, these questions are not even on the radar.

I never asked these questions until Tony, my father-in-law, suddenly died. I only had a little over two years to get to know him. Tony and I met at a time when I was finally taking my faith seriously and beginning to grow. Tony became a mentor for me. I watched how he responded to stress, family, finances, and church and saw an amazing example of a Christian life. Six months after my wife and I married, Tony suffered a stroke. Within hours we were standing next to his hospital gurney. Half of his body was paralyzed but that did not stop him from sharing a laugh or two with us. He informed us that he just had a CAT scan and we could inform our beagle, Tyler, no cats were found! I believe he used humor as a way to comfort us in the situation. Even in the midst of this fearful moment, Tony thought of others first.

It wasn't long before I was sitting in the hospital chapel. I prayed for Tony to be healed and spared so he could see his future grandchildren (I assumed there would be grandchildren). I prayed God would spare him because there was so much Tony added to the world on God's behalf (I assumed to know Tony's place in God's plan). I prayed Tony would stay because there was so much I needed to learn from him. (I just wanted him to stay for me). Less than twenty-four hours after the stroke, Tony passed away. I was angry. This was a great man. He almost always put others before himself. He was a servant and a leader. He took being the "hands and feet" of Christ to heart. Why would God let this man die? Why did God allow so many scoundrels to live well into their eighties while this saint died at forty-seven?

During the days following Tony's death, I heard a pastor say to the family, "God doesn't make mistakes." That was the pastor's brusque attempt to comfort the family. When I heard the statement I had to physically distance myself from this man for fear I may scream at him or worse. In chapter six, I discuss things not to do when trying to comfort others. It certainly is true a perfect and all-knowing God does not make mistakes, but what did that have to do with Tony dying? Was the pastor claiming God killed Tony? Was the pastor saying God stands behind the heavenly curtain, like the Wizard in Oz, pulling levers and pushing buttons, some of which bring death? Did it happen to be the day God pushed Tony's button? "God does not make mistakes." Tony's father responded to the pastor's statement with, "God may not make mistakes, but He sure came close this time!" I could not tell if this response alerted the pastor that his theological ism was not helpful in the midst of a family's grief. Ironically, the pastor's statement made me search harder into the sovereignty of God. God sovereignly used this statement to influence my choice to search harder for Him

## ASK BEFORE TRAGEDY COMES

Even in Tony's death, he still mentored me. His sudden departure brought on a slew of questions. I knew Tony would not want me to simply ask the questions in anger and then forget about them when emotions subsided. I knew he would want me to search for answers and I have been ever since. I read and studied Scripture and any book I could find on the subjects of God, suffering and what the Christian faith offers. Tony's tragedy set me on a path, which helped prepare me for the tragedy of my daughter's diagnosis almost seven years later. I learned theological truisms – like the one the pastor offered Tony's family – seem cruel and indifferent to us when our emotions have been flayed and laid bare. This is not to say the truth should be denied simply because the emotions have reached a crescendo. It simply reinforces the point we need to explore our understanding of God and suffering before tragedy comes. We need to explore our understanding of God and prosperity as well. Let the intellect ingest the truth, so the heart has time to digest the truth, so we can respond to circumstances and not simply react. Truth can bring comfort and wisdom once we have had the opportunity to process it. That process can begin before tragedy strikes, before tragedy further skews our relationship with God. The process can begin right now so if blessings come or have come, they will not overshadow our relationship with God or be wasted.

However, the truth can be hard to bear. Losing a child is hard to bear. How can we bear "The LORD struck the child" if it is true? Could this ever bring comfort? What does it tell us about the God who in other verses of Scripture is described as love? The story of David and the death of his baby boy can cause us to stumble in our trust of God and Scripture. But if God is really whom he says he is, if he is all knowing, then certainly he can handle any questions we have for him. The real question becomes, "Are we ready to hear any of the answers he has for us?" We must understand God neither owes us answers nor is he compelled to give any explanations. However, in his grace he has provided the answers we need.

As we explore these answers, we must be aware of our intent and presuppositions. We must be aware of how these preconceptions can either cloud or clarify our understanding of God's answers. It is difficult to accept our lack of sovereignty. It is difficult to be fully aware of how ingrained culture's influence is in our thinking. It is difficult to get out of the habit of thinking purely from a perspective trapped in time and space. It is difficult to escape our egocentric tendency. But as difficult as it may be, the journey is worth it. Our hearts and minds long for the answers this journey provides. I have found some of the answers were not what I expected and I have found the answers to questions I had not even thought to ask. I have found more questions. As we face our circumstances today and in the future, we need these answers to be more than a theological thesis or stated belief. We need these answers to materialize in our lifestyle, choices and words.

## SELF-ASSESSMENT

We must honestly answer the following questions. It does not matter if we are facing a major tragedy, major victory, or just the daily grind. These questions need answering.

1. How do you define a blessing from God? Is it "things going my way?"
2. What motivates your choices of how you spend your time, money and energy?
3. What do you control in your life? How do you respond when things are out of control? Anger? Puzzlement? Depression?
4. Do you believe God is real?
5. Do you consider beliefs and spiritual things less real than the physical world around you?
6. Thinking of your current circumstances, how far reaching are they? (Think beyond just the immediate people involved. Consider future generations and events.)
7. Are you a child of God? How do you define what this means?

## 2

# The Lord Struck The Child

*The Story of a Baby Boy*

When we were pregnant the first time, we learned during an ultrasound we needed to choose a girl's name. My wife wanted to know the gender before delivery because she is a nurse and wanted to be prepared. The soon-to-be grandmothers wanted to know beforehand so they could start shopping for baby clothes! The first girl name I liked was Caitlyn but Jennifer would not settle on any name. We had the exhaustive name-your-baby book where we could peruse every name and what it means. We browsed that book endlessly. Jennifer made lists of names she liked and even wrote down a few boy names for the future. We actually picked out Jacob's name before his big sister was born! I grew more and more concerned as the pregnancy progressed. My wife is a shopper at heart and she has to survey every option before she makes a purchase. Choosing a baby name was no different. On top of that, she is rarely punctual. I was worried our daughter would be born without a name.

There is a nameless child mentioned in 2 Samuel 12. The story does not explicitly state how old this child was, but we get the impression he may have only lived seven days. Hebrew boys were named eight days after their birth on the day of their circumcision. If this boy died at seven days old, it might explain the absence of a name. In spite of the brevity, this child's life had impact and a purpose. In order for us to understand his life we must know the story of his parents. We must see what circumstances led to his conception, birth, and death. We must see the motives that led to those circumstances. We will ask God about the cosmic-level cause and effects behind this story.

The most famous story of David in the Bible is that of his battle against Goliath. Second is David's sin with a woman named Bathsheba. David's life story is marked by two famous moments, a victory and a fall. However, most of David's life and career as king of Israel was productive and honorable. The prophet Samuel referred to David as "a man after God's own heart." (1 Samuel 13:14) Granted, this declaration came before David was actually king and fell into this sin with Bathsheba, but Samuel was speaking under God's inspiration. From before the foundation of the world, the omniscient God knew everything David would do. God knew David would trust him most of his life. God knew David would defeat Goliath when others fled in fear. Likewise, it was no surprise to God David would be disobedient. David should have been on the battlefield when Israel's troops went to war against the Ammonites, but he stayed in the comfort of his home.

## MESSENGERS OF NOT-SO-SECRET SECRETS

It was no surprise to God that while David was away from that battle and on the rooftop of his home, his eyes would catch the image of beautiful Bathsheba bathing below. Ironically, Bathsheba's husband, Uriah, was away faithfully serving on the battlefield. David sent for her and they had an affair. She became pregnant. To cover up the affair, David tried to orchestrate a sequence of events to bring Bathsheba's husband home from battle and sleep with his wife so everyone would assume the baby was Uriah's. But Uriah would not go home and be with his wife because he was dedicated to God and his comrades. He would not indulge in the comforts of home while the Ark of the Covenant was housed in a tent, as were many of the people of Israel and Judah. Even a human king does not have complete sovereignty over his subjects. David, the leader of the nation and commander of armies, could not even orchestrate a date night for a young couple! When David's cover-up failed, he schemed to have Uriah killed through battlefield maneuvers. David became a murderer in an attempt to conceal the fact he was an adulterer.

But it was not a total secret. David utilized several of his servants to enact his schemes of adultery and murder. David sent servants to bring Bathsheba to him when he initiated the affair. One of the servants even tried to warn David to stay off this path by reminding him that Bathsheba was already married. (2 Samuel 11:3) After the tryst, Bathsheba "sent and told David, and said, 'I am pregnant.'" (11:5) This means she sent word by a human messenger. When David put his cover-up in motion, he used messengers to bring Uriah in from the war. When Uriah would not sleep with his wife, David sent him back to the battle carrying a sealed message to commander Joab. The message was to carry out the murderous, battlefield maneuvers. Ironically, Uriah was the messenger of his own death! Joab was commanded by David to purposefully put Uriah in the line of fire. This was adultery and murder by messenger.

It would be reasonable to guess some form of a rumor mill existed in the palace. The messengers could have put two and two together as these events unfolded. They would have seen David bring Bathsheba to the palace. Then they would have seen a message arrive from Bathsheba two to four weeks later when she realized her pregnancy. Of course the message could have been secret and sealed if it were even written, but it was most likely a verbal message. At the very minimum, they would have at least known the source of the message. Shortly thereafter, the servants witnessed David suddenly remove Bathsheba's husband, Uriah, from battle and spend an unusual amount of time with him. Then they saw David send Uriah back only to hear Uriah's death reported a short time later. The servants then observed the king's cold response to the death of the man who just days earlier was David's drinking buddy (2 Samuel 11:25). After Uriah's death, Bathsheba went through a period of mourning, possibly seven days, and David brought her to his house and made her his wife. She had a baby boy seven or eight months later. Certainly, some in the king's court could have noted these events and been suspicious of David and Bathsheba. The greater populace of Israel may have been unaware of these events. But there was One who knew the secret and situation best.

God sent another messenger into the mix. God sent a prophet, Nathan, to confront David about his escapades. Nathan used a creative approach to re-sensitize David's conscience to the evil in his life. He told David a parable of a rich man who owned many sheep and a poor man who only had one. In the story, the rich man took the poor man's sheep in spite of the poor man's love for his one and only lamb. David became enraged over the story and his anger "burned." He stated the rich man deserved to die but instead of death the man must pay fourfold for the lamb since he showed no compassion. (2 Samuel 12:5-6) Nathan responded to David, "You are the man!" No, Nathan did not make this statement in our modern sense of praise to brag on David's judicial abilities. Nathan showed David how he was the rich man in the story. David had many wives, but he took the one and only wife of Uriah with no compassion. David was not a livestock thief, but an adulterer and murderer. Nathan let David know his scheme was no secret to God. This carried serious ramifications. Under the Law of Israel, David deserved death for his actions.

## TRUTH, JUSTICE, AND THE…ER…BIBLICAL WAY?

We are reminded of the need for justice when we watch the news and hear stories of heinous crimes. It may be easy to stay detached with stories on the news, but when tragedy comes closer to home, our desire for justice can "burn" within us. Even those opposed to the death penalty struggle with their position when it is their child that has been murdered. They struggle with it because of the need for justice. Societies need penalties for criminals. Legal penalties deter criminal activity to some degree, but once the crime is committed those penalties become more than a deterrent to the next would-be criminal. For the victim, those penalties become a source of justice.

The victim's immediate need is to see the criminal "pay" for what was done. Deterrent is a distant second concern, if it is a concern at all, for the victim. If an obviously guilty criminal gets a "not guilty" verdict simply because of a legal loophole or technicality, we can often feel justice was not served. The plots of many movies and books have been based around a victim seeking their own justice when the court system fails. Those stories are popular because we want to see justice served and the guilty pay. We do not want the bad guys to "get off scot-free." Notice the terms we used to describe these situations. Criminals must "pay" for their crimes. The word "scot" in scot-free is an old term referring to a tax or payment. We say phrases like, "He paid his debt to society," when a criminal finishes his prison sentence. We view justice as something owed and paid like debt. So, if crime creates a debt to society, what kind of debt does sin create with God?

This is obviously one of the areas we struggle concerning our concept of God. We approve of justice when we are the ones enforcing it, but we get nervous when God wields ultimate justice. For decades now, our culture has increasingly embraced a relativistic view of morality claiming there is no absolute truth or right or wrong. The idea is a society, group, or individual should decide what is true for themselves. This, of course, impacts our sense of justice. If individuals or groups, independent of others, determine truth and morality, then we have no stance to label the actions of Bin Laden, Capone, or Dahmer as immoral. The Hutus in Rwanda simply determined for themselves the Tutsis were a problem for society and they set out to get rid of the problem through genocide. Of course, the Tutsis were working from a radically different view, or morality. So, how do we determine which group's "morality and truth" should prevail? Once we begin to determine which one is better, we suddenly find we are comparing both the Hutus' "truth" and the Tutsis' "truth" to an ultimate truth. Relativism ignores this obvious truth and that is why it is ridiculous and self-defeating. Relativism makes the Rwandan genocide morally acceptable!

We have ultimate truths and it is upon those our justice system should be based. It is upon those absolute truths we decide murder is wrong and lying is despicable. Based upon those ultimate truths we know there is a need for justice when the threat of legal penalties do not deter. Where do we get these truths? Where does our "moral law" come from? It did not come from a Darwinian process, for human history shows if morality were left to itself to evolve, it would have gone extinct long ago. The fact we can even discuss the issue shows us there are bedrock moral truths upon which we fall back. If there is a "moral law," then there must be a moral lawgiver.ᵛ The Bible reveals God as that lawgiver. To be perfectly clear, murder is wrong, but not because the Bible says so. Murder was wrong before Genesis was ever written. The Bible simply reports the truth murder and adultery are wrong. The Bible reveals God's view of evil and the fact evil is a direct rejection of him and his character. The Bible did not invent this morality, but reports the eternal reality that God is good and anything contrary to him is not. The Bible is the necessary source of truth we need because we live in a fallen world. However, as exemplified by relativism, we tend to resist the truth.

## RECOGNIZING TRUE BOUNDARIES

Once Nathan the prophet confronted David on his sins, David responded with, "I have sinned against the LORD." David knew he had violated God's moral law, which was revealed in the Torah, the first five books of the Bible and foundation of Israel's legal system. However, notice David did not say, "I have broken the law." He did not say, "I have offended the customs and values of others." He said he sinned against God. He contradicted God's character and morality. David did not respond with relativism or situational ethics. He did not respond with legalism and search for a legal loophole to get himself out of the charges. He was fully cognizant of the clear, stark line he crossed. He was aware he had offended a perfect and holy God. By law, by God's own decree in Leviticus 20:10, adulterers were to be put to death. According to Leviticus 24:17, murderers were to be put to death. According to God's law, David should have been killed for his crimes. But he realized the sinful track he was on and stopped. He changed directions and came back to God. This means he stopped committing adultery. He stopped murdering. He stopped "blaspheming" the LORD with his actions.

The word repent is what we use to describe David's action here. From a biblical standpoint, repentance is not simply saying "sorry" and feeling remorse. It is also changing our minds and hearts to agree with God's view. It is recognizing first and foremost we deserve justice for our sins, and sins are not "mistakes." David did not make a "mistake" when he committed adultery and murder. Mistakes are when we give the wrong sum to a math equation or double the salt in a recipe. No, David chose to do wrong and that was sin. We are so fond in our culture of labeling sins as mistakes. It softens the blow to our conscience and is much more comfortable than owning up to the evil choices we make. As long as we call them mistakes, we will never see true change in our lives. Christ did not call us to repent of our mistakes, but of our sins. The first step in repentance is to recognize the wrong we have committed and the next step is to turn away from those wrong decisions and make choices that are inline with God's truth. Repentance is not an emotional state, but a changed person. David repented. God forgave him and said David would not die for his sins (2 Samuel 12:13).

But notice David repented before he knew what God's judgment would be. He did not consult with Nathan about the legal ramifications and if there was a way to soften the punishment. He did not ask for any plea bargain. David knew the law required his death and he repented anyway. He could have decided to run to a distant country and not face the punishment for his crimes. He could have said, "Well, I've blown it anyway so I might as well go all out for as long as possible." David did not go into further rebellion. He repented, ready to accept the consequences for his actions. Just as David made Uriah the messenger of his own death, God made David the messenger of his punishment. David's judgment of the fictional rich man in Nathan's story became the judgment David faced. He would not die, but pay four-fold for his crime. The fact God would "take David's sin from him" (2 Samuel 12:13) and not require his death was quite a surprise. But what Nathan told David next was a bombshell, especially for us as modern readers.

## DID GOD CROSS THE LINE?

Throughout the Bible, we can find descriptions of God's righteousness, love, patience, justice, mercy and goodness. But what God did next seems to fly in the face of all those descriptions. God's action in the following verse made me not only stumble, but fall on my face. Nathan said:

> However, because by this deed you have given occasion to the enemies of the LORD to blaspheme, the child also that is born to you shall surely die." So Nathan went to his house. Then *the LORD struck the child* that Uriah's widow bore to David, so that he was very sick. 2 Samuel 12:14-15 (emphasis added)

The Lord struck the child! How does this phrase legitimately exist in the Bible? How can it align with the Bible's overall description of God?

I am perplexed even further by the poem this whole situation inspired David to write, a poem we refer to as Psalm 51. David states, "Be gracious to me, O God, according to Your lovingkindness, according to the greatness of Your compassion blot out my transgression." (Psalm 51:1) Where was God's lovingkindness and compassion for Bathsheba's child? We can grasp justice. We can grasp the concept David committed several immoral acts and deserved penalties for such. What we cannot grasp is how justice was served when the child was sentenced to death and David was left to live. But it is in there. It is included in the Scriptures for all to see. If we believe God inspired the Scriptures, then we believe they are inerrant and must be handled accordingly. We would have to believe God wanted this phrase included in the Scripture for us to deal with and learn from. I believe God, being God, can handle any questions we throw at Him. We just need to assess if we are really ready to hear the answer. Some of us are not. I was not for a long time and there are still aspects of this for which I am not ready. I think God put verses like this in the Bible to make us ask questions. Verses like this can make us dig deeper and to know him more.

There are a few points to note about the original Hebrew text here. There has been debate among scholars if the phrase about the "enemies of the LORD" blaspheming was truly in the original writing. This is important since we believe it was the original writings that were inspired and inerrant. By the way, the phrase "the LORD struck the child" is unquestionably part of the original writing. Modern translations are attempting to covey this inspired and inerrant message as accurately as possible.[vi] The idea is that the text was changed to say David caused the enemies to blaspheme instead of simply saying David blasphemed (see the ESV). But it makes little difference in this case if the original was written with the phrase or not, for either way it is true. When David sinned, he became an enemy of God and his actions in fact were "blasphemous" or "contemptuous" toward God. Paul the Apostle wrote of this truth and refers to sinners as "enemies" of God (Romans 5:8-10) and James the apostle wrote if we live according to the values of the world, we make ourselves "an enemy of God" (James 4:4). David's actions also gave occasion for any skeptics or nonbelievers to blaspheme God by what they saw David do. This would seem to indicate David's sins were not as secret as he may have thought. The scandal may have been revealed to the public by this point if the "enemies" knew about it. However, the enemies referred to may have been closer to home.

How many hypocritical Christians do we know? Do we see one in the mirror? When our walk does not match our talk, it is very noticeable. Christian or not, all of us fail to live up to our own standards at some point. We contradict our stated values and beliefs with our actions. For those who claim to believe in Christ, this double life gives plenty of reason for nonbelievers to mock and continue in disbelief. The Irish evangelist, Gypsy Smith once said, "There are five Gospels. Matthew, Mark, Luke, John and the Christian, and some people will never read the first four."[vii] When our walk matches our talk, we become a powerful witness. When it does not, we lead others away from Christ. David's sins, the sins of Christians, are blasphemous and stir blasphemy in others. Our hypocrisy is never as concealed as we think.

## Cardboard Reflections: Blog for October 23, 2006

Macayla is continuing to do well with school and she does more for her teachers than she will for us at home. She eats foods for them she won't for us. She interacts in ways there that she won't at home. She is being like most kids; she puts on a show for others but not for us. That is comforting. She's a five year old after all!

Macayla's condition sunk in the other day, as it sometimes does. These are times when the reality of her condition and prognosis comes to the surface fresh and full of pain. I started thinking about how Macayla would go to heaven before we will (barring any unexpected departure on our part!) But the thought occurred to me, "Has Macayla seen enough of Jesus reflected in me to recognize Him when she sees Him?" I know that Scripture says that one day every knee will bow and every tongue will confess that Jesus Christ is Lord. So, everyone will "know"

Him when they see Him. But as one preacher said, some of those knees will be scraped, as they are left no choice but to finally admit that Jesus is Lord. But at the heart of my question was that when Macayla gets to heaven will she see Jesus and say, "Oh, hi Lord, it's you. I saw your reflection in my family. How great it is to see you fully now."

But then I thought about the fact that all of us are "terminal." We will all die at some point regardless if it is at 12 or 92. Will my son recognize Jesus when he sees him because of what he saw in me? Will my wife? Will anyone who meets me? I'm ashamed to say that I'm a poor mirror. I feel about as reflective as cardboard most days. But it is the Refiner's fire that gets the impurities out of the precious metals so that they reflect the Refiner's image more clearly. I hope that I will surrender to that purifying work. I pray Jesus' reflection will shine a little more each day.

The original text in 2 Samuel 12:14 transliterated begins, "because of this blasphemy you blasphemed…" and ends with, "the son born to you to die he will die." Blasphemy, blasphemy, die, die. In Hebrew, repetition can communicate emphasis. David "utterly blasphemed" and the child will "surely die." It is the same way God told Adam and Eve they would "surely die" if they disobeyed him. But in the case of Adam and Eve, their physical death was delayed. The initial death, or separation, they experienced was separation from God's presence in the Garden of Eden. David deserved justice, but the way God enacted this justice is puzzling and even horrifying from our perspective. The child's death was not as delayed as it was at the Garden.

God's actions can seem even more puzzling when we consider the Law he gave Moses. The first five books of the Old Testament are considered the Law, or Torah, and it was from this David, Nathan and all of Israel operated from in these situations. Deuteronomy is the final book in the Torah and it was written in the ancient form of a suzerainty treaty. The suzerainty treaty was between a powerful king and a weaker kingdom. Instead of destroying the lesser kingdom, the overlord king would layout in the treaty what was expected of the lesser kingdom as well as what the overlord king would do in return. Deuteronomy follows the pattern of a suzerain treaty and laid out laws and statutes the Israelites were to follow.

As with most treaties of this type, Deuteronomy also has a section listing blessings and curses. Blessings were promised if the Israelites, the lesser kingdom, followed the Law. Curses were promised if the commands were disregarded. God's actions with David's child were puzzling when we consider one of the laws listed in Deuteronomy. Deuteronomy 24:16 states, "Fathers shall not be put to death for their sons, nor shall sons be put to death for their fathers; everyone shall be put to death for his own sin." Did God violate his own command by putting this nameless child to death for the sins of David? Did God violate his own treaty with Israel? In light of all the controversy in our day over abortion, how can we claim it is wrong if God killed this baby? What grounds does anyone have to claim God wants us to preserve life when he struck the child? In short, is God faithful?

This is where our human perspective reveals a common misconception. This command from Deuteronomy 24:16 is directed toward the Israelites. They were not to extend the prescribed legal penalties of a crime to the criminal's family. Each criminal was to be punished for his or her sin. This was not a proclamation that God's judgment was limited in such a way. This may sound like legal maneuvering, but the fact is God gave the Law to humans for humans to follow. It reflects the character and morality of God, but it was not a formula prescribing exactly how God would act in all situations. It prescribes human action. From our limited perspective, we tend to project upon God our limitations and restrictions. We tend to think God should be held to the same standard as us. We can miss that if God is the all-knowing, all-powerful, perfect and good Being who created everything, then he actually is above the standard. We do not apply a standard to him, but he applies one to us. There are portions of the Torah where God describes what he has committed to do, but Deuteronomy 24:16 is not a command for God to follow, but a command for the Israelites to obey. So, does that mean the standard we are to follow is all children born out of wedlock are to be killed? Does it mean a parent's sin will bring death to their children? No.

We must remember an infinite and all-knowing God gave the Law to finite and ignorant humans. God put it in human language and he was fully aware of human language's beauty and limitations. We lack the knowledge and wisdom to fully understand God, but we have enough to know him and his desires for our lives. He has not told us all truth, because we are not capable of handling it in our present condition. But he has told us all the truth *we need* in our present condition. Certainly, an all-knowing God is cognizant of exactly how much of the truth we are capable of handling. Thus, there must be a reason "the LORD struck the child" was included in Scripture. We must also remember this story of David's unnamed child is descriptive and not prescriptive. It describes what happened at a point and time in history and does not prescribe what will happen to every child born to sinful parents. If God killed the children of every sinful parent, the human race would have gone extinct with the first couple.

## THERE IS MORE TO THE STORY

In spite of knowing this, I still struggled with why God would strike any child in any situation and bring about that child's death. Shortly after the diagnosis, I was watching Macayla have multiple seizures. She was in her bed and it was striking how she appeared to be possessed. It is understandable why people could confuse demon possession with epilepsy. It is even more amazing that New Testament writers differentiated the two conditions (Matthew 4:24). Watching helplessly as my daughter convulsed with glazed, far-away eyes, I began to weep. I buried my face in her bed and wept in prayer, "Why? Why? Why? Why?" Unexpectedly and softly, I felt Macayla's hand on my head. I looked up. She was not seizing but looking right at me. She was there, not glazed over and distant. In an attempt to comfort her sobbing Daddy, she placed her hand on my head. Macayla responded to my pain in spite of her limitations. But I wanted to know how God who is unlimited responds to my pain. I wanted to know if God struck my child. In light of God's ultimate sovereignty, is it proper theological language to say God struck my child? How can I trust him if he did? Again, is God faithful? How can I not be angry?

Looking to Scripture, we find part of the Law describes some of what God may do. There is a list of blessings and curses promised in Deuteronomy. In Deuteronomy 28, God explained that if the people were careful to obey his commands and statutes they would have blessings overtake them. They would be blessed in the city and in the country. Their offspring would be blessed, their produce would be blessed, and their herds and beasts would be blessed. Their "basket" and "kneading bowl" would be blessed (verses 1-5). Conversely, if the people turned away from God and broke his commandments, then their offspring, herds and produce would be cursed. Even their "kneading bowl" would be cursed (verses 15-19). God promised Israel if they obeyed the Law and turned toward him, they would find protection and blessing. God equally promised if they turned away from him, they would find destruction and death. These blessings and curses were for the group as well as an individual. This is difficult for us as modern, westerners to accept, as we are quite fond of our individualism.

David's sin brought curses upon his offspring in ironic fulfillment of his judgment of Nathan's rich-man story. The firstborn to Bathsheba died as a baby. If we read on, we discover David's other children brought the curses promised to fruition. Amnon was David's firstborn son through a wife other than Bathsheba. Amnon schemed and raped his half-sister, Tamar. This may or may not be connected as a play on words, but Tamar was raped after she kneaded dough for Amnon. "Cursed shall be your basket and your kneading bowl."[xviii] Tamar's brother, Absalom, schemed to carryout revenge on Amnon for the rape. This started a civil war, which temporarily displaced David from Jerusalem. Absalom was killed in the ensuing combat. David's fourth son to die, Adonijah, also attempted to overthrow the kingdom before David's death, but failed. He was later executed. In all, four of David's sons died and one daughter was raped. "Cursed shall be the offspring of your body…" Again, we must remember the death of David & Bathsheba's child in the Bible is descriptive and not prescriptive. In this story, God carried out the curses promised in the covenant he made with Israel. This may show us the "enemies of the LORD" who David caused to blaspheme were indeed close to home. They were David's adult sons.

This may not offer us much comfort if we come away with the view that God reacts mechanically to sin as prescribed in the Law. However, God is not reacting mechanically. In fact, it is probably inaccurate for us to think of God as "reacting." From the perspective of an all-knowing, sovereign God, he would not have to "react" to anything. Being eternal would afford him a simultaneous perspective of all space-time, past, present and future. It is similar to a novelist who lays out the entire plot in his mind before he writes the book. The novelist knows the characters because he created them. He knows the circumstances because he orchestrated them and knows how the characters will react and interact. The problem with this illustration is that it is ultimately fatalistic. In reality, God's plan is predestined, but not fatalistic. Unlike the scripted characters of a novel, each of us has a degree of freedom to make choices and we are each responsible for our choices. Fatalism removes this freedom and responsibility, but the providence of God's predestined plan liberates us to become what we were meant to be if we are his.

This is an important distinction to make. Without choice, we could never understand concepts such as love and justice. God wanted us to experience love, but he would not force this experience. Love ceases to be when it is forced or preprogrammed. Of course, with choice comes the risk someone may not choose the love of God. This happens everyday and the result is evil. David chose to love himself more than God, Uriah, or even Bathsheba. His relationship with her began with lust, not love. In spite of this choice, God did not mechanically react and strike David dead on the spot. However, God did not waste the situation and its resulting circumstances.

## REASONS vs. RESULTS

Earthly circumstances do not drive God's plan, but God's plan drive the circumstances. Obviously, we can recognize a chain of events in our lives leading to a tragedy or blessing. To quote the popular 1980's song by the Fixx, "One thing leads to another." How do we assess our life-changing moments, be they calamity or fortune? Often we wait to see the results of that moment. We look at the results rippling out from that situation and being a culture that searches for the positive and pragmatic, we look for the most favorable result and decide it must have been *the reason* for our tragedy or blessing. We never want to consider the possibility a negative result could be the reason. We simply look at the chain of circumstances and events and judge for ourselves the meaning behind it all. Why do we think we can come up with cosmic-level answers purely from circumstantial-level clues?

Shortly after we received our daughter's diagnosis, some well-intentioned people told me this would make me a better pastor one day. Maybe that is true, but if I had to choose between my daughter and better pastoral skills, I choose my daughter. Some of the folks who made this statement appealed to circumstantial, silver-lined results as the reason for our daughter's death sentence. There are many circumstantial results stemming from our daughter's life and death. Why would one be the reason any more than another? Some of the results are negative yet we are tempted to focus on the positive results as the only reasons for this tragic situation. One of the negative results of David's affair with Bathsheba was God struck the child and the child died. Another negative result was David's other sons followed in his footsteps of lust and murder. This led to Israel's civil war and scandals for the throne. Could God use any of these circumstances in his greater plan? In fact, if we are willing, we can see how these circumstances will point us to some possible cosmic reasons for God striking the child.

This unnamed child had a purpose in his short life. Many messengers were utilized in this story and this little one was also a messenger. This little one, this innocent, died for the sins of others. But he was not simply a target of divine wrath. He served as a message and example of God's justice and mercy. He created a response in his parents that would impact the remainder of redemptive history. His death may have separated him from David, but not from God. His death also prevented David from being separated from God. David turned back to the Lord. This child's death also saved God's people. Had David died for his own sins, the nation of Israel would have most likely disintegrated. It was obvious David's other sons were already corrupt and competing for the throne. Their corruption was not an instantaneous result of David's sin. They were products of ongoing, long-term depravity.

Here we see God weaving David's choices and his sons' choices into His plan. They brought civil war to David but fortunately failed. David's absence would have certainly contributed to the nation's destruction. This nameless child's death was God's judgment, yes, but it was a judgment that preserved God's people and their identity in Him. The child's death played a part in the family line that would lead to Christ. For after his death, David went to Bathsheba to comfort her and they made love. The result was Solomon. Solomon later sat on the throne because the other possible heirs had reaped the consequences of their corruption. God did not let these negative results go to waste. Like David, Solomon had righteous moments and sinful falls. But he built the Temple of God in Jerusalem and it provided the cohesion Israel needed as they struggled to center their culture and nation on God's presence.

These circumstances and the motivations behind them stemmed from and were part of the larger cosmic plan. They all pointed to a bigger, cosmic reality. The implications of this child's death reached as far as Christ. The nation of Israel was preserved and it was in this context Christ came. This child's death played a part in the greater cosmic plan for mankind's redemption. This does not mean we are happy about the child's death. This does not keep it from being a tragedy, but we can have joy that God redeems. The tragedy of this child can reassure us God will not allow suffering to be useless. He will use it to bring about good, even if God causes the suffering. Many Christians have found comfort in Paul's inspired assertion, "God works all things together for the good of those who love Him and are called according to His purpose." (Romans 8:28) If a person does not belong to him, as in they are not "called", then that person will not share in the good as they have rejected the redemption offered by Christ. Did this child, who lived and died before the time of Christ, share in the good? Some scholars have claimed this child was never part of God's covenant people since he was never circumcised and named. This view would lead us to think the child was not only separated from David and Bathsheba, but from God as well.

The Romans text is not saying God is working just good things together, but "all things" together, good and bad. He works them together for the "good of those who love God, to those who are called according to His purpose." We often forget to read the rest of the verses after Romans 8:28. God works good stuff and bad stuff together for the good of people he has always known, whom he wants to conform to the image of his Son (v. 29). God has an ultimate plan for his people (v. 30). If we belong to Christ, our circumstances will never be outmatched by his love and power (v. 31-39). This text never asserts Christians are exempt from suffering or evil in this world. It tells us we are to be defined by who we are in Christ, not our circumstances. Therefore, we cannot simply look at this unnamed child's short life and tragic circumstances and assume he missed out on the good of God's plan. This child's missed appointment on the circumcision table did not exclude him either. Look at end of the story of Jonah. It ends with God's rhetorical question to the prophet, "Should I not have compassion on Nineveh, the great city in which there are more than 120,000 persons who do not know the difference between their right and left hand, as well as many animals?" (Jonah 4:11) God's convicting question shows us He is not capricious. Should God not have compassion on David's child who does not know the difference between his right and left hand? Yes, the child was separated from David, but not God.

## EVIL'S TUG ON THE THREADS OF CREATION

My daughter and David's son can both be seen as victims of a fallen world. It did not have to be this way. God originally created a universe where humanity could choose to sin or not to sin. But sin entered the world through human choice and brought death with it. The universe was created with an economy that requires death to pay for the debt of sin. Had sin never entered, the universe's economy of death would have never been activated. Death, or separation, comes in a few forms. The story of Adam and Eve demonstrated this economy when God warned the couple if they ate the forbidden fruit, they would "surely die." They ate the fruit, but they did not fall over dead on the spot. The immediate "death" they experienced was a separation from God and his fellowship. They died a physical death later.

Eternal death occurs when a person is separated from God for eternity, otherwise known as Hell. Temporal, physical death became part of creation once sin entered into humanity. Adam and Eve could not unlearn sin. Their choice to sin not only affected their relationship with God and one another, but it affected their relationship with the rest of creation. Humans were created as part of, not separate from, creation. God wove the tapestry of creation together and a couple of the strands involved humanity. When humans came unraveled in sin, it pulled on the rest of the tapestry. Everything began to unravel and things began to breakdown. Disease, pain, anger, selfishness, rot, parasites, tornadoes, and more became part and parcel of creation's experience. This has carried on through all generations.

Our genome and brain chemistry has been changed. Our daughter's disease was caused by a genetic mutation and is just another example of the breakdown of creation. The astonishing part of this breakdown is that it is not worse. One molecule changed on a strand of DNA in one of my genes. Another molecule changed on a strand of DNA in the same gene in my wife. Our daughter got a copy of both genes. Two molecules were changed and our daughter died. If it is this easy for her to be afflicted, how are we not all dead from mutations? How has the human race survived this long? Considering all of the factors that must be in place for a healthy baby to be born, it is a wonder, no a miracle, we exist. Our daughter is a victim of this fallen world. We all are. The nameless child of David would have died at some point even if God did not "strike" him. How long will anyone live? The fact most of us live as long as we do is in my estimation a miracle.

## THE TAPESTRY OF CREATION PRESERVED

The source of that miracle is God. The human race has thrived longer than modern medicine has been around, so we cannot take credit. God is the only one who can give life and he is the only one who has the right to take it away. Thus, we have the expression "playing God" reserved for people who take life according to their desires and whims. However, God does not seem to act on whims. If God is all he claims to be, is it possible he knows better than anyone when taking a life is justified? The apostle Paul addressed this in Romans 9 as he quotes from Exodus 33:19,

"For He [God] says to Moses, 'I will have mercy on whom I have mercy, and I will have compassion on whom I have compassion.'" (Romans 9:15) Paul shows that God is the only one who is justified or qualified to plan people's lives. He is the only one who knows how long a life should be, for he made it.

This has comforted me for David's unnamed child as well as my own. Though death separates these children from us, it does not separate them from God. His compassion brings them into his presence once they are no longer in ours. If he preserves creation in spite of the effect our sin has on it; if he preserves humans in spite of our self-destructive nature, then maybe he is the only one who can know which lives are best spent on earth for the most amount of time. Who are we to determine how long and in what capacity anyone lives? If God created humanity in his image and has gone to great lengths to preserve creation in spite of the unraveling tug our sin has on it, then should we not find that reason enough to preserve life as well? God will have mercy on whom he will have mercy. I believe David's unnamed child shared in the "good" of God's plan in spite of being born before the time of Christ. If David died, this child would have been born to a widow mother, orphaned in a crumbling and corrupt nation. Instead, this baby went into the presence of his heavenly Father, a child of the eternal kingdom.

The next questions I want to ask are, "Well, if God is interested in preserving life, then why doesn't he heal our daughter? Why didn't he spare David's son and find another way to bring justice to the situation?" Certainly, an all-powerful God could intervene in every tragedy. He could stop every illness. He could stop every hurricane. He could stop every crime, accident and disaster. But since sin has entered the world and started the unraveling of creation and humanity, when would it end? God would have to constantly intervene and does on many levels. The fact that healthy babies are born every day is just one example of Christ holding all things together (see Colossians 1:15-17). In fact, it is his intervention that has restricted the unraveling of creation into utter chaos. But this common grace of preservation does not solve the root problem. If he intervenes on every little problem, he would be treating the symptoms and not the disease. Thus, the apostle Paul told the people in Colossae that Christ is the way in which all things will be reconciled, by the blood of his cross (Col. 1:18-20).

God's intervention is evident, but he does not create heaven on earth by fixing every problem that comes along. Evil exists, but it can only go so far. "Why has he not healed our daughter?" Maybe we should be asking, "Why was our daughter born to us?" Maybe we can be thankful she even exists and did not die at birth. Why was our daughter's form of Battens disease slower in its progression than it could have been? Because of that slower progression, Macayla experienced many happy moments with us. She experienced the pleasures of pasta, Ranch dressing, ketchup, cheese, and her favorite sauce, Zax sauce, from the Zaxby's chain of restaurants. She played on the beach and in the ocean. She swam in the lake with us. She kept her memory and sense of humor for a long time. She hid from me once when she was still able to crawl. I panicked when I could not find her and began calling for her. Her intent to trick me became evident when her giggle gave away her hiding place under the comforter. She laughed when her little brother would get into trouble. We have many precious memories, which would have never existed had it not been for God's intervention and preservation.

## Good Days, Bittersweet Memories: blog for January 14, 2009

Macayla has had a good couple of days. She has had pretty good bladder function, not perfect, but good. She has fewer secretions and even went to school today. She is worn out it appears, but fairly happy. Hopefully, the next few days will at least stay in this trend. She gets to see her GI doctor and nutritionist tomorrow for a check-up. Hopefully we won't add any calories to Macayla's diet. She is already a heavy load to lift...

I have been scrubbing through some old home videos I shot back in 2005. We got the camera then to try and video a seizure for the doctors. If there was a market for documentaries on Macayla's seizures, I'd have it cornered. It seems that my camera is always looking for a seizure. Anyway, we played the first tape back on Macayla's television so she could hear it. She really listened and laughed appropriately. We forgot so many things. We forgot that Jacob (2 years old at the time) could not say Macayla's name so he called her "La la". We forgot how Macayla would act out her falling spells. She would say, "Whoa, whoa, whoa..." and sway from side to side. She loved to wear her ballerina outfit and run around in it. Jacob loved to kiss everyone then just like he does now. I have shots of Macayla looking back at me in the rearview mirror and laughing. The beach, the lake, birthdays, horses, cats, dogs, flowers, butterflies, Disney World, tea parties... at this point it seems impossible to edit any of it. Unfortunately, they don't make DVD's hold that much video. So, I will have to edit.

But we will always have the tapes and the memories. My favorite memory I saw multiple times on one tape was Macayla looking at the camera, sometimes up close and other times at a distance, and calling, "Daddy!" That will not be edited at all.

There are many possibilities for how our daughter's life could have unfolded, but it progressed along only one of those possibilities. Her life was preserved longer than it would have been in other situations or even in other parts of the world. Our limited perspective prevents us from knowing all the ways God may have intervened in our daughter's life. We are only aware via circumstances of a small portion of God's mercy on us. Through the revelation of Scripture we know God's mercy is infinite. I think we would be amazed to discover how far reaching his compassion has truly been in our situation, even in details unknown to us. We must guard our hearts and minds in the midst of pain so we do not miss the Lord's presence and mercy. We can be completely blind to his grace because of our anger, hurt and grief. We can quickly see this happening if we find ourselves asking the question, "What if…" or making the statement, "If only…" "What if" questions are only helpful if they put *what is* in the proper perspective. Rarely do they accomplish this.

Instead, we must remember the Lord is near (Phil. 4:5).

Why does Paul write, "the Lord is near," to the Philippians? Because they are like us and can forget that simple truth. Since the Lord is near, we can be anxious for nothing and in prayer and supplication with thanksgiving let our requests be known to him (4:6). Because of his presence and our access to him, his peace, which surpasses all understanding, will guard our hearts and minds in Christ Jesus (4:7). Instead of thinking "what-if" questions, we can focus on "whatever is" truths. Whatever is just, whatever is pure, whatever is lovely, whatever is commendable, whatever is excellent, whatever is worthy of praise; not only to ponder but to act on these things and the God of peace will be with you (4:8-9). These few sentences of Paul's letter began with the Lord is near and finishes with the God of peace being near. In between is the truth of his mercy and the power to guard our hearts and minds, even in pain.

The Lord struck the child. But thankfully there is more to the story. It was not arbitrary and cruel. It was not whimsical. It was not pinpointed cruelty either. In fact, mercy and compassion can be seen once our perspective is broadened. We need to acknowledge the fact none of us live in a vacuum and each of our lives sends ripples around the globe and through history. The nameless child of David was a liberator and beacon. His short life led David back to God and saved a nation. Our daughter has also led us closer to Christ and we cannot fathom how far the ripples of Macayla's life will reach. In the midst of this tragedy, God has shown himself to be faithful and given us hope. His peace is with us. We cannot see how it all fits together at this point, but we see his abiding love for us. "For now we see in a mirror dimly, but then face to face; now I know in part, but then I will know fully just as I also have been fully known. But now faith, hope, love, abide these three; but the greatest of these is love." (1 Corinthians 13:12-13)

When we were pregnant with our daughter, it took some time to settle on a name. I discovered and suggested the name Kayla, but my wife said she liked Michaela. I thought she said "McKayla" and wondered if were about to deliver a happy meal! However, Michaela comes from Hebrew and means, "Who is like God?" Once she cured my ignorance, I insisted on a more phonetic spelling to avoid later teasing in school. Thus, we settled on Macayla. We called her Mac for short. But the meaning of the name reminds us that no one is God, but God. It reminds us that he has a purpose and plan for every life. It reminds us that not being God is often the hardest truth for us to accept about ourselves. In fact, our lack of acceptance on this point can fuel the fire or our anger and grief. Trust in God often comes only after we have walked through those flames.

## SELF-ASSESSMENT

1. Do you believe the Bible is truly the inspired, inerrant word of God?
2. How do your beliefs about God and Scripture impact the way you live *each* day? Do people know you as just "a nice person" or do they see a Christ-follower?
3. Do you think God actually uses bad things as part of his plan? Do you believe it is possible that the will of God may include something bad happening in your life?
4. How often do you find yourself thinking, "If only…" or "What if?"
5. What do you think or expect God is like?
6. Do you see your existence as a blessing of God's common grace or a curse?
7. Are you a child of God? How do you define this?

3

# Mourners Strike Back

*The Story of a Grieving Parent*

I was in the room, holding my wife's hand as our children were born. I gave my daughter her first bath. I cut my son's umbilical cord. I held them, changed their diapers, and gave them kisses. Of course, the kisses came after the bath! They spent as many of those first postpartum hours with their mother and me as possible. When Macayla was born, I was shocked to learn the meconium, otherwise known as the "first stool," actually was the first, second, third, fourth, fifth and sixth stools! King David did not experience these "bonding" moments and I may be a bit envious that he missed those "first stools." I am so thankful that I got to be there when my children came into the world. David's experience was much different. He was not able to be in the room with Bathsheba and the child. He did not cut the cord, change diapers, give a bath or hold his boy. If the child was only seven days old, David had little or no contact with the child. According to the ceremonial laws in the Torah, Bathsheba and her son were unclean for seven days after the birth (Leviticus 12). To avoid becoming unclean himself, David limited his direct contact with the child and his mother during that time. Yet, he was not completely uninvolved. The news his child was going to die brought him before God.

## COMING TO OUR END

This distance did not reduce David's grief or concern. David pleaded to God for the child, fasting and laying on the ground all night (2 Samuel 12:16). The child's illness brought David back before God. How many parents have been in a situation like David? Endless days and nights in a hospital's neonatal intensive care unit, where little ones lie helpless and often attached to more machinery than people. Everything becomes touch and go and anxiety mixes with hope; the dread of loss competes with the desire to bond. The very fact these emotions are competing with each other often brings on guilt. However, the Law, not neonatal equipment, impeded David from holding his child.

It sounds strange to us, but the ceremonial laws of cleanliness were followed to prevent the spread of disease, but more importantly to remind the Israelites no part of their lives was separate from their faith. God is holy and perfect. He is without blemish or fault. He wants us to be holy as well. Our sinful condition makes us unholy and this distances us from God. The laws in the Old Testament regarding "cleanliness" help us see the distance and difference between humanity and God. In order for someone to go to worship or participate in offerings, they had to shed the world first. The common had to be removed and the holy put in its place. There were decrees for washing and becoming clean for many of life's common activities. Conception and childbirth were no exception. Making love made a couple "unclean" and they were to wash afterwards and wait until sundown before they were "clean" again. Women's menstruation and childbirth also demanded cleansing rituals. This does not mean menstruation or sex between a husband and wife is naughty. These decrees had health benefits, but most importantly they kept people's faith front and center in the midst of daily life. Even our sex life is to be enjoyed within the scope of faith. Faith was not meant to be a separate compartment of life, tucked away until it is convenient.

David broke the Law and set his faith aside when he committed adultery and murder. By the same Law, David became isolated from his child and new wife when the baby was ill. Convicted of his sin for violating the Law, he would not manipulate it or sidestep it anymore, so most likely David never laid eyes on the newborn. Consequently he could not help the child directly. He could only turn to God. When all of our options and abilities reach their limit, we reach newfound humility. How often we make God plan B when dealing with our struggles. It is unfortunate most of us only come to this humility after our stubborn rebellion fails, but thankfully forgiveness through Christ allows us to come back to him even at that point.

## Prayer on the Porch: journal entry July 7, 2007 (not posted on the blog)

Yesterday, Macayla was a little more agitated and I was busy with things, but not productive. Macayla spent most of the day in her chair or bed. I felt bad because I had not spent much time with her. We danced to the music at the end of Shrek and she seemed to get into it. She smiled and even moved her feet in a way that was quite different than her attempts to walk. I believe she really was trying to dance. But her stomach contents went dark brown again. She had no diarrhea today. Maybe it's back up. She became irritated late in the afternoon so I rolled her out on to the front porch and she seemed to calm down. I was moved to pray for her. I looked at her and she is so beautiful. Her eyes, her hair, her skin all are so pretty. She is so beautiful and she suffers so. I prayed that God would heal her. I prayed that he would put her brain back together. I prayed that she would talk again, eat again, walk again, and see again. I prayed that she would get her hands back and her coordination back. I prayed that God would heal and restore her. Two hours later she began to cry. She cried more than she had a couple of weeks ago. Tears streamed down her face. Her facial expression matched the action. We couldn't tell if she were in pain or having trouble seeing. I think she was in pain and was looking around trying to figure out what was causing it. She seemed scared and hurting. All I could think was, "Hell of an answer to prayer." She went to sleep when I got her to bed and snuggled with her. We gave her pain medication and she eventually drifted off. Around 2 a.m. this morning she woke up crying again. I lay with her until around 3:30 a.m. and she calmed down and went to sleep. She woke up around 7 a.m. but quickly drifted off again. She grinned at me slightly in that moment. God, what are you doing? What am I doing? Macayla is suffering so much. We have been spared the crying for the most part, but when she does it, it kills me inside. I can't keep this up. I'm at my end and I don't even know how to rely on You anymore. Help me. Help Macayla and end her suffering. Please.

David was humbled, turned to God and prayed for the child. This is also interesting considering God had already said through the prophet Nathan the child would die. David knew the prognosis. Did he actually think he could change God's mind? In fact, David told his servants, "While the child was still alive, I fasted and wept; for I said, 'Who knows, the LORD may be gracious to me, that the child may live.'" (2 Samuel 12:22) But God did not change his mind. The child died and much to the surprise of David's servants, David arose, cleaned up, went to worship in the Tabernacle and then came home and ate. The fasting and mourning typically began, not ended, after a death. Notice David worshiped upon hearing the news of his child's death. How?

<u>Old Journal: journal entry for April 11, 2007 (not posted on the blog)</u>

I was entering old journal entries and came across two: one from 10/20/05 and another from 11/03/05. In the first, I wrote about the reality of our universe and what Jesus does and is. I quoted Isaiah as quoted in Matthew. Jesus took on our infirmities and carried away our diseases. It reminds me of Easter and I pray that Jesus will show me my infirmities. Carry away this anger and lack of love that I exhibit when Macayla is screaming nonstop like she is right now. The second entry was about Macayla being healed. I made a statement that I would praise God from the rooftops if He healed her. Now, I am convicted and encouraged to praise Him even if He doesn't heal her.

## DO YOU BELIEVE THIS?

About a month before we received our daughter's diagnosis, I was listening to a sermon on John 11. This is the story of Jesus going to the funeral of his friend, Lazarus. Lazarus had been sick and his sisters, Mary and Martha, sent for Jesus during the illness, but he did not come. He purposefully waited until after Lazarus died. Four days after Lazarus was dead and buried, Jesus finally arrived. In that time and culture, funerals lasted for days so the mourning was still going strong. Mary and Martha, witnesses to Jesus' healing of others, reacted much like we would; much like we do. They basically said, "Where were you? If you had been here and done something, our brother would be alive right now!" Jesus responded to Martha with "I am the resurrection and the life; he who believes in Me will live even if he dies, and everyone who lives and believes in Me will never die. Do you believe this?" (John 11:25-26) As I listened to the sermon on this story, I suddenly became aware God was preparing me for the diagnosis. Just as he allowed Lazarus to die, he would allow my daughter to die. It was as clear as the day a month later when the doctor informed us. I knew my daughter was going to die.

Like David, I prayed and prayed. I lay on the floor and wept. I cried out to God hoping this was not true and somehow our daughter would be spared. All I could think about was Macayla playing in her favorite pink ballerina tights. I saw her wearing the hair band that had two antennae with little butterflies on the tips. I thought of her little giggle that could suddenly burst into a cackle. I thought of how she kissed her stuffed animals with an exaggerated "Mmmwah" sound. I thought of her sense of humor, dry and full of pranks, like my own. I thought of Mac as a baby, snuggled into my arms against her silk, blue blanket and "passy" in her mouth. Image after image of my little girl filled my head as I lay on the floor weeping and praying. Why would God let her die?

But another image entered my heart and mind. It was a scene from the book *The Chronicles of Narnia: The Magician's Nephew*. Aslan, the Christ figure of the story, was with the children in a playful and joyous time. Lewis described it as if the children were being submerged or enveloped in Aslan, as if his great mane was all around them. I pictured Mac there. Once again she would run and she would be at the great feast eating by her own strength. Maybe she would have all the cheese she would ever want. She would need no help in getting the food to her mouth. She would climb the steps with ease taking three, four, or five at a time. She would smile and her eyes would be alive again. She could play with Jesus. Jesus reminded me of his words, "I am the resurrection and the life. He who believes in me, though he dies, will live." Macayla may die, but Christ has her in his hands. She would either be healed with us for a short time, or she would be healed with him forever.

One month later, the doctor confirmed what God had already disclosed. We still prayed for healing. We prayed for a miracle. Many others prayed with us. In spite of Christ's reassurance of Macayla's ultimate wellbeing, we wanted to change God's mind. No matter how hard we prayed, her brain still shrank and her abilities still faded. No matter how many people prayed, the disease still progressed. Why did Jesus heal others but not our daughter? "Jesus, where are you? If you would show up and do something, my daughter would not have to die!" Through listening to the sermon, Jesus also reminded me he is the resurrection and the life. Even if Macayla dies, through him, she lives. Did I really believe this? Could I, like David, worship this God?

David and I are both men of faith, but I could see something more clearly than him because I am on this side of the cross in redemptive history. David was told his sins were the reason his son would die, but God never showed me my daughter's disease was punishment for my sins. To be clear, like David, I had sinned in spite of my faith, but punishment for those sins was handled at the cross of Christ. My daughter's death could not atone for my sins and they did not have to since Christ's death and resurrection already had. Understanding this truth was very sustaining for me. I cannot imagine the guilt David must have felt knowing his child's death was a direct result of his sins. Losing a child is a horrible experience and there are plenty of opportunities for guilt. David's must have been crushing. But that did not stop him from doing all he could for his child. He fasted and prayed. It was the only thing he could do.

After the child died, David did not throw up his hands and say, "Oh, well. God ignored my prayers. I guess He's really mad at me." Instead, much to our surprise, David cleaned up, changed clothes and went to worship. Even David's servants were confused.

David plainly stated, "But now he has died; why should I fast? Can I bring him back again? I will go to him, but he will not return to me." (2 Samuel 12:23) David could not bring the child back to life but he would one day join his child in death. In spite of being on the "front" side of the cross, David was reassured by God's ultimate plans and promises. He was reassured enough to worship the God who just took his son. Sometimes we will refer to the deceased as someone "God took." I am not sure this is always an accurate description, but in the case of David's child it was very accurate. God struck the child and the child died. This is the God David goes to worship! It was before the cross, but David could say, unlike Martha above, "Yes, Lord, I believe this."

## CHOICES BEYOND OUR CAPACITY

Like David, our mourning started before the funeral. We had a prognosis of death and we mourned with every step that brought the end closer. When Macayla had a feeding tube installed in her stomach, we felt we were taking a big step toward the end. But in retrospect, it was early in the process and it was a blessing as it made her life more comfortable. Each time she lost abilities or suffered a new symptom, we felt closer to the end. Every seizure, every vomit, every MRI made the prognosis fresh and real. We did what we could for our daughter and faced the dilemmas new medical advances have created for families with a terminal loved one. Medical interventions can prolong life far beyond what would have been possible even a half century ago. However, can and should are not always one and the same. Each medical intervention we had to consider not only made the prognosis palpable, but it also made us question how far to go with such interventions. If we fought to keep her alive even after her brain shut down, would it be for her or for us?

Most children with Battens disease die from some form of respiratory failure. The intervention is to insert a tube down their throat into their lungs so a respirator can breathe for them. Later the tube is removed to see if the child can breathe on his or her own power. This can happen several times and eventually some children get a tracheotomy and respirator to keep them breathing.

We had to ask ourselves how many times would we intervene like this? These interventions would not change the prognosis. Was there an ethical difference between withholding intubation at the first sign of respiratory failure as opposed to waiting to remove life support later? If we intervened, how many times would we keep sticking tubes down her throat? Would it be for her benefit or ours? These were the realities we tried to prepare for after the diagnosis. Like David, we had to turn to God for help. These choices were beyond our capacity. Our hearts broke to think of the future awaiting Macayla and our family.

But the past also opened the wound of a future we would not have. My wife and I both experienced moments that came with sudden memories of Macayla's early life. We would watch home videos of her running and talking. We could see memories of her working a VCR and television correctly at the age of two. She would pretend the baby-bottle brush was a toothbrush, though it was ten times as big. Those moments brought on the renewed realization of our daughter's status. The running, playing, and hand-eye coordination were slipping away. The pain could come when others spoke of what their children were involved in and it reminded us how Macayla would never do the same things. I once heard my wife reminiscing about the dance she shared with her father, Tony, at our wedding. She cherished the memory and especially since he died six months later. As she spoke, all I could think about is how I would never dance with Macayla at her wedding. I would not see her turn into a woman. I would not see her become a mother. These realizations were markers along our journey of grief.

## THE STUPOR OF GRIEF

Grief is a surprising experience. C.S. Lewis described it well in the book *A Grief Observed*. He said, "No one ever told me that grief felt so like fear. I am not afraid, but the sensation is like being afraid." He goes on to write, "And no one ever told me about the laziness of grief…I loathe the slightest effort." He describes grief with feelings such as "being mildly drunk or concussed," and "There is a sort of invisible blanket between the world and me." He states, "I not only live each endless day in grief, but live each day thinking about living each day in grief."[ix] I first read this book as part of an assignment around the time Macayla was born. Its impact was tenfold when I read it again after the diagnosis. Grief made me feel disconnected from the world around me. I had days that dragged on and every second passed in languid tedium. There are other days I cannot even recall except as a mark on a calendar. My memory, diet, rational and critical thinking, joints and muscles were all affected. My grief caused physical pain brought on by stress and possibly depression. The pain was real and debilitating some days. Deep grief takes us off guard and when it does, our hearts convulse with emotion and our minds become comatose. Deep grief is stupefying.

It is in this stuporous state we find ourselves asking God, "Why?" We ask the question while drowning in the confusion and bewilderment of our emotions. We scream at heaven but we only get silence for an answer. Why would God not answer when I asked him, "Why?" This word and question, "Why?" became an obsession of sort, and at times a battle cry in my anger toward God. As mourners we strike back with angry questions. We shake our fists at God. We wonder how this could happen to *us*. Again, our perspective gets smaller. We struggle to see past the limits of space and time, our lack of sovereignty, and our egocentric tendencies. The net effect can lead to a crushing depression. The emotions take over and our intellect is muzzled. Our minds and hearts both want the answer to "why" but our emotions prove to be stifling to our intellect's ability to absorb any answers. I suffered from this grief. Even as a believer, God's word became difficult, if not impossible to digest on the simplest of levels at times. It would sound foreign or empty. Grief is not something you just "get over." It cannot be reasoned away. It cannot be explained away. I could not even pray it away and believe me I tried.

All of my physical symptoms landed me in the doctor's office. All of my tests came back normal and there was no physical explanation for my symptoms. My doctor and I determined it was possibly related to depression, but I was not a clear-cut case. It was suggested I start an antidepressant to see if it helped. As a believer, I struggled with the idea of taking medication for depression. The physical symptoms I experienced were intense enough to hinder my ability to care for my daughter. If they were psychosomatic, then treating the depression would alleviate the symptoms. But as a believer in Christ, should I not have enough faith, hope and trust in Him to avoid the need for medication? I wondered why God's grace was not sufficiently addressing my depression. This led me to question my faith and even salvation. Did I really belong to Him? Did I really trust Christ's work on the cross? I heard people quote the prophet Isaiah stating, "it is by [Christ's] wounds that we are healed." Was I really trusting in the "healing wounds" of our Lord to heal my depression, or whatever it was? I prayed about it. I asked God for direction and wisdom about starting an antidepressant. The answer: silence. Finally, I told my doctor I would try it and it was not long before my physical symptoms subsided.

After I started an antidepressant, my thinking became clearer. The stupor and fog of grief began to recede. I was able to function again and care for my daughter. I was able to study and pray with focus again. It did not erase any of my questions, but the process of searching for answers was not strangled by emotions. However, I must confess that I did not truly make an informed decision. Had I to do it again, I would have sought true counseling first. I should have sought help through a biblical counselor who could help me find clarity in God's word. Under their care, I might have been able to confront my thoughts with clear, biblical principles and possibly find physical relief, provided my symptoms were psychosomatic. The medication did not erase the questions and it did not get me out of the process of grieving. It simply held me together for a while so I could function on a daily basis. In our culture where pragmatism is truth, this is seen as a healthy victory. However, popping a pill can mask problems instead of solving them. Eventually, I faced those emotions full on when I came off of the medication. Eventually, I still had to seek counseling. Medications are not a substitute for dealing with our feelings, stress or even sins. I will discuss this more later. However, during the time I was on the medication, thoughts and feelings found new clarity.

## LIFTING THE FOG

With the return of clarity, I realized God's blessings to which I had been blind. In spite of becoming a one-income family, we made it each month and our needs were met. Our daughter's situation brought us into contact with amazing people and other families with special needs. We found support from them and could offer support to others as well. We found moments of pure joy with Macayla as she began to laugh more and smile more than ever before. Because of her condition, we were blessed with a memorable trip to Disney World through the Make-A-Wish foundation. We would have never been able to go on that trip otherwise and Macayla smiled more in one week there than she had the six months prior. To our surprise, the larger-than-life characters did not frighten her. She gave Pluto, Shrek and every Disney or Universal character a kiss and many with the exaggerated "Mmmmwah" sound she liked to make. It was a great experience. I was able to see past the emotional fog and realize all these blessings afresh. But it may have been possible to find the same relief and clarity through counseling. Of course, all of these blessings were simply circumstances and there would have to be more to God than things going our way for me to worship him in the midst of this.

There was more. I was able to see Scripture's reassurance again and I found there was an ultimate healing promised in the wounds of Christ. My daughter would have that healing. She would either be healed while she was with us or when she was with Christ in heaven. I knew her short life would impact others and draw them closer to God. I knew this because it was drawing me closer to God. Scripture reassured me every life has purpose regardless of length or afflictions. Macayla's life, afflicted and short though it was, had purpose. We started a website to keep family and friends up to date. We started it so that we would not have to repeat the same story twenty times with everyone. But we soon discovered more strangers and friends were keeping up with it than family. The website became a ministry outreach to share and help other special-needs families, be their needs medical or spiritual.

God has a great purpose and plan and Macayla played a part in it. God's presence and provision was something we experienced in our circumstances and our relationships. Even our family was drawn closer together. There was promise of restoration, ultimate and full. Finally, we realized God was the only one who could do all of these things. He was the only One who could be mindful of such small and finite creatures such as ourselves and still be the infinite, all-powerful and holy God above all things. It was for this I found I could worship God again. My daughter drew me closer to the Lord. In 1874, Reverend William M. Taylor wrote:

> There was a man that had a flock of sheep, which he wished to remove from one field to another and better pasture. There was one sheep refused to go, and ran hither and tither. The man did not stop to follow the sheep, to drive and force it through the gate. No, but he took her lamb and laid it in his bosom, and carried it in his arms, and the sheep followed her bleating lamb and was soon safe and happy in the sweet, rich pasture. So it has often been, and the words of the prophet have had a new verification, "A little child shall lead them."

Taylor then goes on to remind his readers that he, in fact, lost his daughter. His last view of her was when he was leaving in a carriage.

> Years ago, when I was leaving my Liverpool home to fulfill an engagement in the city of Glasgow, the last sight on which my eye rested was that of my little daughter at the window in her grandmother's arms. As the carriage drove me away, she waved her hand in fond and laughing glee, and many a time during my railway ride the pleasant vision came up before my memory, and filled my heart with joy. I never saw her again! The next morning a telegram stunned me with the tidings of her death; and now that earthly glimpse of her has been idealized and glorified, and it seems to me as if God had set her in the window of heaven to beckon me upward to my eternal home.[x]

The unnamed child had a purpose greater than his father, David, could have known. My daughter's purpose was greater than I know. God works through these children to lead us to greater truth, though it is hard to bear. I often wondered if I knew beforehand my wife and I carried the Battens gene, would we still have had biological children. Would I like to avoid having a child with a deadly disease? Yes. Would I have avoided bringing Macayla into this world knowing what I know now? Absolutely not! As much as I detest her life was one of suffering, she is still Macayla and unique. She is not a forgotten and nameless child. Her life affects circumstances, motivations and plays a role in the cosmic realities of God's plan. David's child is recorded without a name, but he was not forgotten. He has a place in Scripture and history. It is a small amount of text and easily overlooked. It would have been easier just to leave the whole story out of Scripture, but God wanted it there for us to read. This should teach us to not minimize the impact any person or event. There is nothing minimal about God's purposes for a life.

**SELF-ASSESSMENT**

1. Is your faith tucked away in a separate compartment, not informing your daily decisions?
2. When facing struggles beyond your control and ability to correct, is God plan B or do you go to him first?
3. What is God's purpose for you?
4. What is God's purpose for your children, spouse, family or friend and how can you encourage and support it?
5. If you find yourself in the midst of grief and depression, would you consider going to counseling before starting medications for depression?
6. Do you think counseling is just for crazy people? When faced with deep-rooted struggles, do you think it is o.k. to seek help, or do you believe you just need to fix it yourself?

# 4

# What Is Truth?

*The Story of a Special-Needs Family*

Shortly after our daughter's diagnosis, we had to start looking for a van that could be modified with a wheelchair lift. We quickly discovered any item with the label "special-needs" cost many times more than other similar items. Special-needs vans cost twice as much as the same van without a lift. Toys purchased for ten dollars at Wal-Mart sold for ninety dollars in a special-needs catalogue and there were no differences between them! During the process of searching for an affordable vehicle option, I met a car salesman who shared he too had a special-needs daughter, but she had died a few years prior. He said it must have happened because of all the bad things he had done earlier in life. He said God was punishing him for the sins of his youth. It was the only time I had a car salesman cry while trying to sell me a car. I was saddened by this man's view of suffering and his feelings of guilt.

Was this man like king David? Was his child struck and killed by God as punishment for his sins? I believe, though I am not God, there is a supreme difference between David's situation and this man's. Remember, 2 Samuel 12 describes David's situation but does not prescribe how every similar situation unfolds. I told this man God's punishment for our sin was dealt with at the cross. For if God punished us for our sin, we would all be dead! Instead, God the Son became flesh, lived a sinless life and shed his blood on the cross to pay the debt of our sin. He not only nailed our debt to the cross (Col. 2:14) but when he rose from the dead, he declared victory over sin and death; a victory he gives to us. When we trust in him as our Lord and Savior, our punishment is handled. It is finished.

Certainly, there is still suffering in the believer's life, but we must not assume this suffering is punishment. Scripture affirms we are subject to discipline from God when we turn toward sin. The writer of Hebrews confirmed God disciplines his people (Hebrews 12). The difference between God's punishment and God's discipline is not merely semantics; the difference is eternity. The car salesman saw his daughter's death as punishment and believed God did not love him. Punishment is done in wrath, whereas discipline is done in love and meant to draw us closer to God. If we assume someone's suffering is punishment, then we risk denying all Christ did on the cross and at the tomb. Unfortunately, this man did not seem to hear what I was saying. He could not seem to perceive the truth that Christ, not his daughter, took the punishment for his sins.

## THE TRUTH IS OUT THERE

Each episode of the popular television series *The X-Files* featured one of three slogans in the opening title sequence. "The truth is out there," became a pop-culture catchphrase of the 1990's.[xi] For all of its post-modern flavor, the show at least posited there was a verifiable truth to be known somewhere…"out there." Do we know truth when we hear it? In our current culture, truth has become an obfuscated concept. Not only has truth been questioned, the concept of reality is questioned as well. Can we know truth? Can we know what is real? As some read these questions they may be asking, "Who cares? I've got bills to pay, kids to feed, and struggles to face." In this response lies the answer to these metaphysical and epistemological questions. You do not need to be a philosopher in an ivy-league graduate school to realize there is a daily reality we all face. Each day has a menu of responsibilities, blessings, pain, decisions, and toil. Certainly, it may feel good to adhere to Eastern mysticism and spirituality and pretend all these things are illusion. However, the phone, electric, and water companies want their illusionary money, as does the grocery store. Those illusions I call children running around my home want their illusionary food to satisfy their illusionary hunger. If, by chance, you actually adhere to a spirituality that declares all of these things to be illusion and find my description of your worldview troubling or disagreeable, then take heart. This book is simply an illusion! For the rest of us, there are many things of which we are certain and it does not take much pressing to recognize their reality.

If we have a close relationship with someone, we can be certain if we love them or not. I am certain I love my wife and children and that certainty is not based on the emotional ups and downs of our relationship. Even when I am frustrated or angry with them, I love them. I cannot empirically prove my love for them in a lab, but I am certain of it. Other members of our family will testify to this love as well, so it is not limited to my experience. When we suffer, we are certain of the pain. This too is not testable in a Petri dish, but it is certain. Then there are the testable realities we live with. Gravity, disease, aging, hunger, and so on. Eastern spirituality and relativism may be tempting ways to dismiss reality and truth, but truth and reality are actually impacting us and do not rely on our belief in them to exist. So then, do we know truth when we see it? Do we recognize truth or do we attempt to create our own reality that is more comfortable? We can "delight in the fantastic but the world of an adult must move from what is merely fantastic to that which is fantastically true."[xii]

## IS GOD A SHOW-OFF?

The story of a special-needs family will help us see how ill founded preconceptions can blind people from seeing the truth, the amazing and fantastic truth. This family lived in Jerusalem two thousand years ago. They had a son, but the son was born blind. Imagine the devastation. Imagine trying to teach the child to feed himself, find a proper bathroom, avoid injury or learn a trade. Most of us never face the challenge of blindness when teaching our children these skills. In their particular culture and point in history, this meant not only heartbreak and challenges around the home, but a future of financial struggle for both the son and his parents. How would he ever be able to earn a living? Occupations for the blind were extremely limited, as in there were none. If he could not earn a living, he would not be able to support his parents when they became aged. They all faced a future of poverty and begging as they advanced in years. Part of their story is recorded for us in the ninth chapter of John's Gospel.

    We get the impression from the story this family not only faced the physical and emotional challenges of this disability, but a spiritual crisis as well. We first meet the son of this family on the pages of John's Gospel when Jesus and the disciples are leaving the Temple. Upon seeing the man, the disciples asked, "Rabbi, who sinned, this man or his parents, that he would be born blind?" (John 9:2) Like the man at the car dealership, they assumed the blindness was punishment for sin, either the parents' or the man's "future" sins. The prevailing theology of the day dictated sinners suffer and the righteous prosper. Sin certainly can bring about suffering as a consequence, but some of the most prosperous people achieve their affluence through sinful means. But that did not matter here. It was assumed this man was being punished for sin. Even the teachers of the Law, the Pharisees, claimed he was "born entirely in sins." (9:34) This man and his family may have spent most of his life with the hollowing and needless guilt thinking their sins brought this calamity. Unfortunately, none of the religious leaders would offer any of the hope found in Scripture to this family.

    In their case, we know their guilt was needless because Jesus clarified for the disciples and us why this man was born blind. Jesus said, "It was neither that this man sinned, nor his parents; but it was so that the works of God might be displayed in him." (John 9:3) Jesus emphatically states it was not sin that brought on this blindness. It was so this man's life would be an example of God's "works." But does that offer us much comfort? Does this mean God is toying with our lives just to show off? Could God not demonstrate his works in ways that did not cause so much suffering?

    This reaction exposes our assumptions and reveals our blindness to the bigger picture. Here our limited perspective and egocentric tendencies show themselves. Scripture describes God's creation process and how upon its completion all was "very good" (Gen. 1:31). There was no indication God created man and earth with the intent of causing strife. However, if God were all-knowing, he would have certainly known what was coming. Sin entered creation when humanity disobeyed God's single command. "Do not eat of the tree of the knowledge of good and evil." There were not even Ten Commandments to follow, just one and it was broken. But we may ask why this tree and commandment were necessary in the first place. Again, without choice, humanity could never experience God's love. Love ceases when it is preprogrammed or forced. For creation to be "very good," humanity needed to experience love and that experience comes when there is real choice. With this choice comes the real possibility humans would choose selfishness over love and that is exactly what Genesis records for us. Humanity chose selfishness, thus the tapestry of creation started unraveling. It was no longer "very good." It not only impacted how we act, but it also degraded genetics, plant life, animals, weather and so on. The fall of humanity has wrought havoc and this is the *real* inconvenient truth we choose to ignore! The true miracle is God did not allow the tapestry to completely unravel.

The man's blindness in John 9 was a product of this fallen world and not his or his parents' personal sin. Jesus clarifies that individual sin does not automatically explain individual suffering. But God will display his "works" in this fallen world. Multiple places in Scripture describe God's works as "mighty" or "merciful" among other adjectives. God's preservation of creation is a miracle as he would have been justified in wiping the slate clean the first time sin entered the picture. But he preserved it instead and even intervenes at specific points to heal, and provides ways the situation can be used to glorify him. We may recoil at this. What, is God a glory-hound? Again, God is not like us. It is not conceit when God says he is holy and perfect because he is in fact holy and perfect. He deserves glory based on who he is and his "works" are ways to reveal this to us. We can be thankful he wants to reestablish the relationship we lost in the fall. These works are part of the revelation of this divine desire and this can actually bring us comfort. He has not left us alone in our suffering, but can actually work through it to reveal his ultimate care and plan for us; and yes, in this he is glorified. Jesus healed this man and his life-long disability became part of the "works" of God's redemptive plan. Can he not use any of our lives in the same way? Can he not take any of us from being a blind beggar of scraps to a generous and radiant mirror of his glory?

# THE FALLOUT

This man's story is not over and we get a rare glimpse into the life of the person after their miracle. The text tells us Jesus spit on the ground and used it to make clay. He rubbed the clay on the man's eyes and sent him to wash in the pool of Siloam. Imagine. He patted the water of the pool from his face with the end of his tunic and opened his eyes for the first time. The impact of the new stimulus was overwhelming. So many sounds he heard all his life now had images to go with them. So many objects he felt all his life now had color and proximity. For the first time, his eyes beheld his own hands, the hands he had used in place of his eyes. Jubilation, timidity and over stimulation mixed in that breath-taking moment. Voices of people he knew now had a face and he quickly discovered they were struggling with this miracle as well. They debated if it was even the blind beggar they had known. This debate was understandable as he certainly acted different and was out of the context they had always known him. He was no longer just sitting and begging.

The people pressed this man for an explanation and he shared how Jesus had healed him. They took him to the Pharisees to try and learn how this fits into what they believe as a community. They turned to their spiritual leaders to gain greater insight into what this could mean. If God is sovereign, he caused this man to be born blind and, at least from their theological understanding, due to his sin or his parents' sin. This meant Jesus, a man from Galilee, just undid what God had done! The people needed to make sense of the situation and they went to the only people they knew who might be able to shed some light: the Pharisees.

As it turned out, the Pharisees were just as baffled by this miracle as the people. Unfortunately they clung even tighter to their theology of divine retribution. They could offer no insight. They were blind while this man could see. But their theology and authority silenced the equally baffled parents of this man. His parents knew it was their son and even testified of his life-long blindness to the Pharisees, but they feared the repercussions if they validated what Jesus had done for their son and family. These parents now had a brighter future because of this miracle, as their son would be able to make a living. Ironically, by embracing the miracle, they now faced ruin because the Pharisees would throw them out of the synagogue and community. This would equally threaten their livelihood. They cowered and turned the Pharisees attention back on their son.

Alone, their son repeatedly explained to the Pharisees what happened, "…one thing I do know," he said, "though I was blind, now I see." But they would not accept this answer. Exhausted by redundant interrogation, the man gave a forceful response, "I told you already and you did not listen; why do you want to hear it again? You do not want to become His disciples too, do you?" They rebuked his sarcasm and assured him they were disciples of Moses, but as for Jesus, they did not know where he was from. The man's response continued, "Well, here is an amazing thing, that you do not know where He is from, and yet He opened my eyes. We know that God does not hear sinners; but if anyone is God-fearing and does His will, He hears him. Since the beginning of time it has never been heard that anyone opened the eyes of a person born blind. If this man were not from God, He could do nothing." (John 9:24-34) The Pharisees excommunicated the man from the synagogue and effectively from the community.

## ARE WE BLIND?

But Jesus found him, explained who he was and the man worshiped Jesus. Within earshot of the Pharisees, Jesus said to the man, "For judgment I came into this world, so that those who do not see may see and that those who see may become blind." (9:39) The Pharisees asked in sarcasm, "We are not blind too, are we?" Jesus' response began with, "If you were blind, you would have no sin; but since you say, 'We see,' your sin remains." He continued his response with a metaphor of sheepherding (John 10) to help them understand his play on words. He conveyed a greater reality than simple, physical blindness and sight.

In the typical style and context of John's Gospel, the characters involved assumed Jesus was referring to physical blindness. John recorded multiple interactions where Jesus was speaking of the full reality of our spiritual condition and the people still thought with a more limited perspective of the physical. When Jesus told Nicodemus a person must be "born again," Nicodemus struggled to understand Jesus was not speaking of the human womb, but the spiritual rebirth he offers (John 3:1-21). We struggle to see a greater perspective at times because we can be so inebriated by our egocentrics, space-time, and sin. But Jesus spoke of the spiritual reality and this should not be considered a lesser reality. The spiritual realities revealed in John's Gospel can include the physical, but that is a small part of the greater whole. Jesus lifts us to a greater perspective in the Gospel of John. He enlightens us, if we are willing, to seek and do God's will (John 7:17).

The struggle of people to know the truth when they heard it is a continuous theme in John. "In Him [Jesus] was life and the life was the Light of men. The Light shines in the darkness, and the darkness did not comprehend it." (John 1:4-5) In the chapters preceding the story of the man born blind, the constant debate rages about who Jesus is and what his teachings mean. Some believed in him. Others debated. Many denied. But Jesus told them to not judge according to appearances, but with righteous judgment (7:24). Unfortunately, most of the people who heard his teaching could not break free of their limited perspective, their tainted theology or their sin in order to hear and understand the truth. He affirmed for them he was the Light of the world and of life (8:12 & 9:5). Utilizing legal arguments, the Pharisees tried to prove Jesus' testimony was false (8:13-20). They accuse him of having a demon while others observe that a demon-possessed person would not say many of the things Jesus said. There is a constant flow in and out of the temple in chapters 7-10 where Jesus and the Pharisees are debating and ironically the truth escaped the most religious people in Israel. Jesus said multiple times his sheep know his voice and by extension this means those who are not his sheep do not know his voice. The darkness does not comprehend the Light (John 1:5).

Interestingly enough, one of the chief complaints of modern readers and skeptics is that Jesus never makes the overt statement, "I am the Christ." Based on this omission, skeptics claim Jesus' teaching was twisted and his divinity assigned to him by later Christians. This point of view has little basis or strength historically or philosophically. It suffers from the same problem the Pharisees suffered. Over and over in John's Gospel, they ask him directly if he is the Christ. He answers them in multiple ways that confirms he is indeed the Son of God. We must realize the phrase "Son of Man" was another way of describing the Christ or Messiah. Jesus used multiple "I am" statements to get his point across. "I am the Light of the world." "I am the Good Shepherd." "I am the door of the sheep." "I am the way, the truth, and the life. No one comes to the Father but by Me." "Before Abraham was, I am!"

To our modern minds, these phrases can seem quite cryptic. To the Jews of that time, these phrases had very clear claims. The phrase, "I am" reflects upon the name of God, Yahweh, which means, "I AM." It was the name God revealed to Moses. It is interesting to witness the irony of modern skeptics denying Jesus ever claimed to be the Messiah. The Pharisees repeatedly asked Jesus if he was the Christ and he responded in multiple ways to say he was. Many of those times they sought to seize and stone him for blasphemy. They wanted to stone him because his answers all claimed his identity as the Messiah. Otherwise, they would have ignored him. Skeptics want to "stone" the Christian faith based on a false understanding of Scripture. The Pharisees and modern skeptics do not know the truth when they hear it. Again, the darkness does not comprehend the Light.

The story of the man born blind begins with a question about the relationship between suffering and sin. At its deepest level, the question is asking for an explanation for the existence of evil. The story begins with a man blind and begging. The story begins with wrong-headed theology and assumptions. The story begins with Jesus giving us a cosmic-level reason for this man's suffering and reminding us He is the Creator.

> Jesus answered, "It was neither that this man sinned, nor his parents; but it was so that the works of God might be displayed in him. We must work the works of Him who sent Me as long as it is day; night is coming when no one can work. While I am in the world, I am the Light of the world." When He had said this, He spat on the ground, and made clay of the spittle, and applied the clay to his eyes, and said to him, "Go, wash in the pool of Siloam" (which is translated, Sent). So he went away and washed, and came back seeing. John 9:3-7

The first thing created in the beginning was light. Light in our universe is a reflection of its Creator. Jesus is the Light of the world, but the darkness, those caught in the darkness of their sin, cannot comprehend Jesus. Just as the creation account in Genesis speaks of God forming man from the clay of the earth, here Jesus makes clay to repair the man's body. Jesus used spit from his mouth just as God breathed life into humans with his mouth. This miracle was about more than correcting eyesight. It is a testimony of Christ's identity.

## NOT OUR DESIGN

While Jesus is in the world, he said, "*We* must work the works of [God]." He did not say "I" but "we" must work the works. Those who belong to Christ participate in the "works" of God. Some of these works are the miraculous, physical healing of broken bodies. Some of these works are the healing of broken hearts. Some of these works share the truth that makes people free (John 8:31-36). We do not always know how these works will happen and what their result will ultimately be. We do not always get a cosmic-level explanation for our circumstances and suffering. But this is where we must trust in Christ, the sovereign God of all, for they are his works. He knew healing this blind man would bring about this man's faith in him. He also knew it would result in the man being ejected from his synagogue and community. We wonder why Jesus didn't both cure this man and preserve his ties to the community. But we are to participate in the works of God, not design them ourselves. Let us not forget that even though a human community rejected this man, he was now part of God's family.

I often asked God to heal Macayla. I prayed continually he would reconstitute her brain and remove the mutation in her genes. He could do it. He is the Creator. For him, rebuilding a brain would be easier than a car company rebuilding an engine. I knew we could get empirical proof of her healing through an MRI and blood work. I bargained with God and gave him my best sales pitch. So many people who had come to know us and our situation would be impacted by such a miracle. It could make national news, medical journals, and could even be a made-for-television movie. The whole world could hear about it and God would be glorified. We could have our daughter back. I prayed, wept and prayed some more.

God graciously heard my pitch, and he convinced me he would heal Macayla, either with us or with him in heaven. Either way, she would be whole again. Even though that is not exactly the answer I was looking for, it began to bring me comfort.

God reminded me the works he wants to do are his and not mine. He knows which would be the greater miracle: Macayla's full, physical healing here on earth or the lives changed by her short life. Both scenarios would have impact, but he knows what will change the world and in the best way. He also reminded me miracles are temporary corrections in a world like ours. If Macayla was healed in childhood and spared an early death, it did not mean she would miss out on death later. She would still die at some point by disease, age, violence or accident. The man born blind received his sight, but this did not guarantee he would keep his sight in old age. Even after his miraculous recovery of sight, he faced the next challenge in his life when the Pharisees excommunicated him. But the blind man's life was used to display the works of God. Likewise, Macayla's life was designed to display the works of God.

The story of our blind man begins with bad theology but ends with him seeing things clearer than ever before. But it also ends with others going deeper into their darkness. The man knew the truth when he heard and saw it. The Pharisees and skeptics thickened the cataracts of their souls. This should be a stark reminder that even in the face of overwhelming evidence of God's miraculous work, people may still refuse to see and know the truth. Even if Macayla's brain were completely restored, there would be many who would still reject God's involvement and existence.

Our cynical and irresolute culture is nothing new. Standing before Pontius Pilate moments before death, Jesus said, "You say correctly that I am a king. For this reason I have been born, and for this I have come into the world, to testify to the truth. Everyone who is of truth hears My voice." Pilate responded, "What is truth?" (see John 18:37-38) The culture of Rome contained so many opposing religions and claims to truth that Pilate had grown cynical and doubting like us. Do we know truth when we hear it? Do we know our Shepherd's voice? We all have the special-need of truth. With truth comes change and that change can be difficult, but freedom is found there as well.

Scripture challenges us to see more truth than we can handle at times. Much like the overwhelming flood of images and stimulus the blind man experienced at the Pool of Siloam, we are going to face a similar flood of knowledge as we explore another story in Scripture where God is glorified in a man's tragedy. Hopefully, as the cleansing illumination of the Holy Spirit washes over our eyes, we will be able to clearly see things we may have only heard in the past. Maybe we can begin to see the path and not just feel our way through life. Maybe we can declare with the man in John's Gospel and the hymn writer, "I was blind, but now I see!" God has not made the truth some mysterious thing that is somewhere, "out there." He gives us the truth we need but it does not come in pill form to be quickly taken and all is known. His truth is a great land that must be explored and experienced. It is revealed to us and given as a gift, to be both trusted and witnessed.

## SELF-ASSESSMENT

1. Do you believe there is such a thing as absolute truth and can you know it?
2. Do you equate bad circumstances in your life with God's punishment?
3. Does it bother you that God seeks to be glorified? If so, what can that reveal about you?
4. Does Jesus sound like He is speaking the truth to you, or does it sound more like "pie in the sky?"
5. Who do you believe Jesus is or was?
6. Are you a child of God? In other words, do you know your sins separate you from God forever and only by trusting what Christ did at the cross and tomb can your relationship with God be restored? Is Jesus the way, the truth and the life?

# 5

# In the Hands of God

## *The Story of Job*

    I just met a family whose daughter was born premature and only lived five days. The father stated he had been living away from Christ before his daughter came. He had grown cynical of church and faith. During the funeral, the father said his daughter had a message and purpose. She led him back to Christ. She showed him, like David, even a brief and afflicted life can lead others back to their Creator. We cannot assume this small child died because of sins she would commit one day or for the rebellion of her father. We can be certain this small child *lived* to draw her father and others to the Savior. It is interesting and providential this little girl's name was Sophia, from the Greek for "wisdom."

    In the Bible, there are several books classified as wisdom literature and Job's story falls into this category. Job is described as "blameless, upright, fearing God and turning away from evil." (Job 1:1) In other words, Job was more than just a nice guy. He gave his belief in God more than just lip service. His daily lifestyle was shaped by faith. He was wealthy and had many children. Job often interceded for his children and consecrated them before God with offerings after they feasted and celebrated just in case they "sinned and cursed God in their hearts." Job was not only their father; he was also their priest. Job continually prayed and interceded for his children (Job 1:5). Kids being kids, Job had a perpetual concern for his children's relationship with God. Job was a good father and a good child of God. He is one of those perfect people; wealthy, wise, godly and a great parent. To be honest, this description of Job can make us sick.

    But the scene changes and any envy we harbor for Job will

soon be replaced by pity and horror. We are given a glimpse into the realm usually hidden from our eyes. Job is unaware of these events, but we are given a moment of access to the court in heaven. Satan came before God. There is no explanation of how he got there or why. He entered and received an audience with the Almighty. In pseudo-naiveté, God asked the "adversary" where he had been. Satan claimed to have been roaming the earth. Then God did a very curious and troubling thing; God mentioned Job to Satan, "Have you considered My servant, Job? For there is no one like him on the earth, a blameless man, fearing God and turning away evil." (Job 1:8) What did Job have to do with this? God dangled Job out in front of Satan like bait and Satan took it, "Does Job fear God for nothing? Have You not made a hedge about him and his house and all that he has on every side?" (Job 1:9-10a) It seems Satan had in fact considered Job before. He admitted Job was out of his reach due to God's protection. Satan wagered Job would curse God if the blessings stopped.

This wager was also a two-sided accusation based on pragmatism. On one side it asserts people will only worship God as long as it benefits them in some way, but not simply for whom he is. In other words, having faith in God is good as long as it "works." Faith is good if it helps someone be balanced, centered or provides any number of psychological or emotional benefits. Of course, if those benefits cease, then it is necessary to move on to some other religion or worldview and see if it works. The other side of Satan's wager asserts God's value is centered on humanity's acknowledgement of him. The story of Perseus from Greek mythology asserts a similar claim, that the gods are nothing without the prayers of men. However, Job's story will utterly destroy these accusations.

In the meantime, God gave Satan permission to strike all of Job's blessings. Satan quickly and abundantly set to work and Job hears the results through four separate messengers on the same day. The first messenger reported Sabean raiders killed Job's servants and stole his livestock. A second messenger reported Chaldeans raiders did the same. Another messenger reported "Fire of God fell from heaven", possibly lightening, killing sheep and shepherds. The final messenger reported great winds had knocked down a house, killing Job's feasting children inside. It is difficult to imagine such a day. Four rapid-fire messages of death and loss would be numbing

(Job 1:12-19). For Job, there was no time to even breathe between messages, much less grieve and adjust. But Job did not curse God! Satan lost the wager, at least for the first round. Round two increases Job's suffering, striking him with anything short of death. Job's suffering is so great that none of us can consider it "small potatoes" next to our own. It was as great and probably greater than any suffering most people experience in our culture. Therefore, we can see Job's suffering as credible and we can learn what it has to offer for our circumstances.

## IS IT GOD'S FAULT?

Because of Macayla, I want to know what light Job's story sheds on God's character. Is he capricious and cruel? Is he unaware of my problems? Does he care? Are we nothing more than poker chips on God's casino table? In anger and grief, I want to know why God "would strike my child." Job eventually feels betrayed by God and we can as well in the midst of our suffering.[xiii] Job's grief and his friends' counsel also jump off the page for me. How would I respond to their counsel? Is there any value to what they are saying? Can Job's responses and speeches help me? The next chapter will consider Job's grief and their counsel. For now, let us focus on God. As the song says, "He's got the whole world in His hands…" But do we want our world to be in his hands?

God struck the child in David's story and it seems God struck Job as well. Many may say it was really Satan who struck Job. We feel compelled to defend God because it makes believers uneasy to blame God for unleashing evil into someone's life. But that is exactly what God did to Job. He unleashed Satan just like a handler lets an attack dog off a leash. God gave Satan permission to kill Job's children and servants and take all his wealth. At first, Satan could not touch Job. God would not allow it. So Satan took everything he had. God unleashed evil and people died. Many people never get past this point. They may say, "See, the God of the Bible is cruel! Why believe in a God like that?" But if someone is willing to go a bit further, they may find there is more to the story and there is more to God.

It is notable none of the servants blamed Satan for the

tragedies and neither did Job. In fact, one servant reported the sheep and shepherds perished by the "fire of God." Maybe that particular servant was an early version of an insurance adjuster and considered the catastrophe "an act of God." Many people today assign all the blame for natural disasters to God, but none of the praise for the miracles in nature. On the other hand, many believers blame Satan for all suffering and evil in their life. It is quite notable in the book of Job that Satan, the adversary, is only in the first two chapters and is silent for the remainder of the story. Instead, God becomes the focus of the debate as to the source of evil and how sin and suffering work in our world. Satan is a real creature who relishes bringing pain into the lives of humans, however we can fall into the trap of giving him too much credit and not recognizing the evil of which we are all too capable. We must realize when we talk about the problem of evil we are talking about ourselves. If the problem of evil is going to be solved, we should be ready to admit our own contribution to the problem[xiv] and that the solution will apply to us as well. Ignoring the reality of spiritual warfare against Satan is just as pleasing to that old devil as when we ignore our culpability and make him the scapegoat. Satan vanishes from Job's story after the second chapter, but Job's human friends adequately take on the role of "adversary" throughout the rest of the story.

In Job's case, Satan is tempting him through pain because in Job's pleasure and blessings, he glorified God. Job's faith in God during times of blessing gave him a better foundation for when suffering came. Job always remembered his blessings came from God and were not simply products of luck or his own prowess. Pleasure is typically where faith is lost not gained, but that is one of the reasons Job is extraordinary. In our case, Satan has been very effective in tempting us in our pleasures so when the pain of suffering comes we are much easier prey than Job. We only ask the hard questions about God when grief or loss hits us in the face. But that is when our intellect is drowning in pain and emotion. When life is more or less going our way, when we are inundated with pleasure, our intellect is alert but the hard questions about God grow quiet. Our blessings and pleasures distract. All in all, we can easily credit ourselves for our fortune and blessings and blame God for our calamity. Job's story is one that will challenge us to see how much we truly put God first. Job was faithful in both his pleasure and his pain and we can learn to be as well.

Nevertheless, we must acknowledge what Scripture affirms in Job's case. God exposed Job to Satan. God's wager with Satan costs the lives of servants and Job's children. Surely the all-knowing God of heaven must have known how Satan would react when Job's name was mentioned. God must have known Satan would wager and ask permission to strike Job. God must have known Satan would incite murdering bands of foreigners to attack Job's lands. God, if he is the all-knowing God, must have known Satan would cause the deaths of people. Yet, God unleashed evil.

## GOD PLAYING GOD

How can we trust a God who would do this? We get upset when people like Hitler "play God" but we get even more upset when God "plays God." It is one thing when a human takes life because we eventually have some chance for recourse. Despots and tyrants can eventually be stopped. But what recourse do we have with God? The story of Job once again awakens the fear God is arbitrary, cruel and he might snatch anyone up at any moment. Job even lamented to God, "Your hands fashioned and made me altogether, and would You destroy me?...You renew Your witnesses against me and increase Your anger toward me; hardship after hardship is with me. Why then have You brought me out of the womb?" (Job 10:8,17-18a) Job essentially asked if he was created to be God's punching bag. He could see no other point to the suffering. Unlike David, Job was not being punished for sin, but the issue of sin drives much of the dialogue in this story. The description of Job in the opening verses by God as being blameless and righteous is important so that we know his suffering was not punishment for sin.

Here is another sticking point for many in our culture. Does God punish? I have heard people say, "I just can't believe in a God who would send people to Hell." They think it would violate the idea of God being "loving" if he sends people to Hell. This is a ludicrous and shallow objection. Unfortunately, it is also ubiquitous. We can simply respond to this objection with an equally ludicrous question. "How can we be a loving society if we put pedophiles in jail?" Why do we think God is wrong for sending sinners to Hell while we are civilized for putting criminals in jail? We think it is our moral right to be angry with God, but cry foul at the very idea God could ever be angry with us. Our culture attempts to turn the very relationship of God and humanity on its head. We want to re-create God according to our standards and reserve the right to live by none ourselves. We want a docile God who is warm, fuzzy, and absent of anger. We, the creatures, want to define reality for the Creator. We want God to exercise justice according to our whimsical ideals and we certainly do not want to admit his sovereignty. If we are going to understand Job's story, it will help to remember Job and his friends never doubt God's sovereignty. They never doubt his just nature, though they may debate how it plays out among humanity. God does not play God; he *is* God.

## LETTING GOD OFF THE HOOK

It will also help us to see two opposing views of God and how they try to solve the problem of evil. One approach to "let God off the hook" is to deny God's knowledge of the future. This position is called Open Theism and is also held by Process theologians. The basic concept is that the future does not exist yet so it cannot be known. Therefore, God can still be all-knowing because he knows all that can be known. The future is simply not part of that knowledge because it does not exist to be known. Open Theists will maintain God has great wisdom and can tell us the best choices to make, but that wisdom is only based on his perfect knowledge of the present and past. This position brings comfort on the issue of evil and a good God because a good God is not leading us into an evil situation on purpose. Of course, this position makes us wonder why Jesus taught us to pray and ask God to "lead us not into temptation." (Mt. 6:13) If God does not know the future, this prayer makes little sense. Open theists assert God is not orchestrating events that will be evil. The most comforting and motivating part of this position is that it means we have "true" freedom. We can choose whatever we want. It means we have more sovereignty over our future, as it is based on our choices and not some pre-destined plan. Granted, those choices can be influenced by God's wisdom, but to live in accordance with his wisdom is itself a choice.

At the other end of the spectrum is a fatalistic version of Calvinism. True Calvinism, named for the Reformer John Calvin (1506-1564) is not fatalistic. Unfortunately, some have stretched Calvin's teachings, and the logical conclusion for their beliefs is the exact opposite of Open Theism. This position holds that God has ultimate authority over every creature and event that has ever taken place or ever will take place. He knows the future perfectly because he has planned it. He has ordained every action, good or evil, and even sustains them. He ordained, planned and sustained terrorists just as much as he ordained, planned and sustained charity workers. He is the source of good and evil. Every choice we make he has ordained, and in this fatalistic version of Calvinism, it means our choices are predetermined. Therefore, even our evil choices are predetermined. Further, we are somehow still responsible for our "choices" and can be punished for them. As far as punishment and responsibility for evil, that is also predetermined by God's will. His elect will be saved and all others will not. God determines who the elect are and human choice has nothing to do with it. The idea is there is no way God's plan could be fulfilled completely unless he controls every detail, down to the last atomic particle. Otherwise, human choices could thwart the ultimate desired outcome. The comfort this provides the believer is that God does in fact "have the whole world in his hands" and anything we suffer will be for the greater good. We can trust a perfect God will work all things together, good and evil, for the good of his elect. Of course, you may not be one of the elect and there is nothing you can do about it!

Open theists often use verses of Scripture that support or demonstrate human choices while doing interpretive gymnastics on verses asserting God's sovereignty and foreknowledge. Likewise, hyper-Calvinists readily attach to verses asserting God's sovereignty and preordination of events and do their own interpretive contortions on Scripture asserting human choice. In an attempt to deal with the various views in Scripture, God's will has been divided and categorized by theologians on both sides. Thus, there is talk about God's necessary will and free will, his secret will and revealed will, or his antecedent will and consequent will. We can choose (unless you are already a hyper-Calvinist!) between a weak God who is not completely sovereign on one end, or a puppeteering, fatalistic God on the other. However, if we believe the Bible to be God's word, inspired by him and without error, then we must believe the same Spirit of God inspired both the verses asserting God's sovereignty and the verses asserting the freedom of human choices.

This in and of itself should give us comfort over Job's story. It was included in the Bible. If the Bible is not the inspired word of God Christians claim it to be, then Job would have never reached its pages in its present form. People from ancient times may not have had access to all the information we do today, but they were not stupid. They could recognize contradiction just as easily as us. Over the past few thousand years, many people have had access to the Old Testament and could have easily changed its contents. They could have left Job's story out or revised the opening chapters so there would be no "wager" between God and Satan. But, just as "the LORD struck the child" was left in Samuel's scroll, so Job's scroll was left in the Bible. This same Bible also records God's love and mercy. Anytime we read a story like Job, it helps to step back and remember it did not have to be in there. If the Bible were merely a human fabrication, its contents would have been harmonized more to human liking. It would have been harmonized to reflect a more unified, theological perspective. Instead, it was divinely crafted and divinely harmonized. Thus, we can be sure it is not a "pie in the sky" rendition, but a communication of reality. It is a revelation of who God is and an honest one that doesn't pull any punches. When we cling to one portion over another, we do not have the perspective intended for us.

## **CHOICES SOVEREIGNLY WOVEN**

The whole of Scripture leaves in tension the truth God is sovereign and the truth humans make choices for which we are responsible. There is a mystery here as to how God weaves our choices into his plan in such a way his plan utilizes those choices without being thwarted or determined by them.[xv] We make choices. Granted those choices are influenced by so many factors including our sinful nature, but they are in fact choices. We are responsible for them; otherwise there would have never been a need for the Law or Scripture. There would be no need for God to give any commandments or reveal his will to us if it was already scripted what we were going to do or not do.

It should also be observed we often think of God planning all that will happen through time in a very linear fashion, linking each event to the next until the end of time. Both hyper-Calvinists and Open Theists assume this is how a God with foreknowledge would have to plan. Each of us has a life story with multiple factors involved, such as genetics, location, illness, personality, era in which we live, etc. Our life story, Macayla's story, is shaped by these factors as well as our worldview, decisions and circumstances. We can see all of this laid out in a chain of events from our birth to our death. Further, our life story overlaps with the life story of others composed of their own factors, worldviews, decisions and circumstances. Billions of people throughout all of humanity's past and future will have their own life story, linking to lives before and after their own and to others around them.

This is but a guess, for I am not God, but it would be reasonable to believe that an infinite, all-knowing, all-powerful Creator of everything could coordinate multiple factors, decisions and circumstances for billions of people on the planet simultaneously in the past, present and future. God's plan could simply account for a range of choices I make as well as a range of choices anyone else has or ever will make and still bring about what he wants. At any given moment, I may face a decision between A and B. God can sovereignly allow me to truly choose between A and B and coordinate that decision with all the other factors, decisions and circumstances with which it will relate. Of course, there are times he may also sovereignly guide me, or even force me, to choose A over B. The bottom line is he sovereignly weaves, or has woven, all human choices into his plan the way he wants and in a way we are incapable of fully grasping.

Consider the Exodus. God called Moses to go back to Egypt before Pharaoh and demand the enslaved Hebrews be released. Scripture states God "hardened" the heart of Pharaoh so that he would not let the Hebrews go. (see Exodus 4:21; 7:2-5) God intervened in the decision-making process of the Pharaoh. We are not told God took over Pharaoh's mind and turned him into a robot. It simply states God intervened in a human's inclinations in this situation to bring about a desired end that was for the ultimate good. This is not to declare the end justifies the means, for we are not fully capable of understanding the means God always uses as in the case of the Pharaoh. This story describes what God did but does not necessarily prescribe what he always does. I believe Pharaoh would not have resisted Moses through all ten plagues if God had not "hardened" his heart. He would have caved in much sooner. But God decided to bring judgment upon Egypt and demonstrate through the ten plagues their gods were false and their ways were evil. The ten plagues were polemics against the gods and spiritual forces of Egypt.[xvi] God empowered Pharaoh's stubbornness to accomplish this. God was not "playing God" but *being* God. How often we forget he is the only one who can and has the right to do so.

Scripture affirms in multiple places the crucifixion was planned from before time began (see Ephesians 1; 1 Peter 1:20; Rev. 13:8). We may assume if Judas had not betrayed Jesus, the crucifixion might not have happened. What if Pilate was sick that day? What if there was a huge storm on that awful Friday? How many factors had to fall into place for the crucifixion to occur when it did? The problem with questions like these is they put God in a box. Do we worship a God whose sovereign plan can be completely thrown out by little men like Judas or Pontius Pilate? Absolutely not! I assert God could make the crucifixion happen and still allow Judas an actual choice. We may also forget the disciples were targets of Satan just like Job. Satan entered Judas. Jesus said Satan wanted access to Peter as well. Both Judas and Peter made choices to betray Jesus. They made actual choices and did not simply follow robotic programming even though their choices were foretold. Their choices were determined, known, ordained and preserved by our sovereign God from before the foundation of the world. Do we understand how? No, and that is why he is God and we are not.

## OVERSTEPPING OUR BOUNDS

Scripture does not explain everything there is to know about God. It reveals what we need to know and exposes where our capabilities of knowledge find their limit. In our fallen and finite condition, some things will remain a mystery and ignoring parts of Scripture that make us uncomfortable does not solve the mystery. For the hyper-Calvinist, it may be uncomfortable to admit humans make actual choices, not robotic functions of a plan. For the Open Theist, it will be uncomfortable to admit they are not sovereign over their future. Dividing and compartmentalizing God's will oversteps our bounds and we run a great risk of becoming blasphemous. "Then the LORD answered Job out of the whirlwind and said, 'Who is this that darkens counsel by words without knowledge?'" (Job 38:1-2) We must move past shallow theology but we must not overstep our bounds.

In Job's case, as in ours, God's sovereignty is clearly demonstrated as Satan can only afflict Job with permission. Even the Open Theists' position offers little comfort here. Look back at the two first chapters. After Satan's first attack, he went back before God in heaven and once again God brought up Job:

> The Lord said to Satan, "Have you considered My servant Job? For there is no one like him on the earth, a blameless and upright man fearing God and turning away from evil. And he still holds fast his integrity, although you incited Me against him to ruin him without cause." Job 2:3

What was that? Did God say, "you incited *Me* against him to ruin without cause"? Did God just take responsibility for Job's suffering? How can God claim Satan "incited" him when it was God who brought up Job in the first place? Certainly, one does not have to know the future to guess how Satan would react to God raving about Job's righteousness. Like us, Satan got sick of hearing about "Mr. Perfect," the goody-two-shoes of Uz. God certainly knew Satan would want another shot at Job. God is considered the source of Job's suffering by everyone in the story, including God.

Here we must be careful. Someone at church once asked me, "Why does God allow Satan to come before him and accuse me and tempt me?" We must remember Job's story is descriptive first and prescriptive second. Many biblical stories describe what happened and do not prescribe what will happen every time similar circumstances reoccur. The second chapter of Acts records for us that Peter preached a sermon and about three thousand people became Christians. This describes what happened. It does not prescribe that every time I preach the Gospel three thousand people will become Christians. Likewise, every time suffering comes into my life it does not necessarily mean there was a conference in the heavenly court between Satan and God. "Have you considered my servant, Jeff? He is not exactly blameless. Did I mention he is easy to tempt into gluttony?" (Jeff 1:8) When suffering comes into our lives, we can remember God is sovereign. However, his plan makes it possible for Satan and us to make actual choices, which carry actual consequences and responsibility. We must not assume God is punishing us for our sin. We must not assume to know more about God than what Scripture allows.

## REAL SOVEREIGNTY, REAL CHOICES

Again, I am reminded of the car salesman I met who told me his special-needs child died as punishment for his past sins. Certainly, God is capable and justified to punish us for our sins. This may include punishment that impacts others as the story of David and Bathsheba demonstrates. But Job's story demonstrates innocent people can suffer tremendously. The man in John 9 was born blind but not due to sin. These stories have one thing in common: God. He is exercising control in all of these stories of suffering. This may anger us because we want him to exercise that control to stop the suffering. We want him to intervene and make circumstances more to our liking. Before we allow our anger to blind us, we need to remember God is not only exercising control in suffering, but he also subjected himself to the same. God the Son put on flesh in Jesus Christ. His suffering and torment was not limited to the ripping of his flesh and the piercing of his body. His suffering was not limited to the suffocating pain racking his body on the cross. His suffering included betrayal. His suffering included having to become sin, even though he never sinned himself. He took on your sin and mine. The weight of the just wrath all our sins deserve was placed squarely on him. His suffering included hellish abandonment on the cross, "My God, My God. Why have You forsaken Me?" (Mt. 27:46, Ps 22:1) In our grief over suffering, we can remember what Calvin Miller sublimely expressed, "Do not be angry at heaven! God also lost a boy. He understands. Don't be mad at Him; rather reach out to Him."[xvii]

This is the God who has the whole world and us in his hands. They are nail-scarred hands. Job was in his hands as well. Job's wisdom and faith are amazingly reflected at the beginning of his story. When his wife, in understandable grief, says, "Do you still hold fast your integrity? Curse God and die!" Job responds, "You speak as one of the foolish women speak. Shall we indeed accept good from God and not accept adversity?" The narrator clarifies for us that in all of this Job did not sin with his lips (Job 2:9-10). Job acknowledges God's ultimate sovereignty even in his undeserved suffering. But he also acknowledges the real choice he faces. Will he trust God even when it seems to make the least sense? This is a real choice Job must make. Job is not following a computer program. He has the real possibility of sinning in his suffering. His suffering and his choices that follow are truly part of God's plan. This plan involves not only Job, but also his wife, friends, Satan and eventually us. We also face real choices. Will we shake our fists in blinding anger or reach for the nail-scarred hands of the One all too familiar with suffering?

Here we discover some of the wisdom Job's story offers for our lives as we face all types of circumstances. Regardless if it is the blessing of prosperity, the mundane routines of life or travesties like Battens disease, we must ask ourselves where God fits in. For some, God is an afterthought. In the midst of prosperity or comfort, God can be completely forgotten and we attribute our success to our own ability. Other times, we may half-heartedly thank him but deep down we assume he was supposed to bless us anyway. In difficult situations, some may only go to God when everything else has failed. God becomes plan B. Others may quickly go to God in their pain as they should, but once life gets back to "normal" God is no longer sought. One of the pearls of wisdom from Job is that God is to be on the throne of our heart in good times, bad times, or anywhere in between. Many Christians will claim that Christ is in their life, but he is meant to be more than just one more thing in our life. He is to be the Lord of our life at all times, in all circumstances, and in all decisions.

## SELF-ASSESSMENT

1. Do you really believe God is sovereign over everything?

2. Can you see that God's sovereignty is not limited by a timeline or human choice? If so, what does it mean for your choices and their impact?
3. When do you get angry with God?
4. When you think of Jesus' suffering on the cross and all of its painful details, how does it change your perspective on your own suffering?
5. Are you a child of God? Is Christ always on the throne of your heart and mind or just when it is convenient?

# 6

# In the Hands of Humans

## *The Story of Job's Comfort*

The only people who can begin to relate what we went through with Macayla are those who went through similar circumstances and even then, no two situations are identical. Other people not facing a situation like ours would say, "Any time I think things are bad in my life, I think of what you are going through and realize I have it easy." Some people go through horrendous struggles that put our common trials of life into perspective. God used Macayla's situation to certainly adjust our priorities and focus. I hope Macayla's life brings perspective to others facing those common trials and encouragement for those in a dark storm of life. But even our situation needs perspective and Job's story accomplished this for me. He lost not one, but seven children all in the same moment and without warning. He lost his wealth and his health. When I look at Job's situation, I know my circumstances could be worse.

However, not everyone gains perspective when someone they know faces calamity. When tragedy strikes someone's life, our oblivious and obtuse comments come out. We heard several comments fitting one or both of these adjectives throughout our journey with Macayla. The comments were well intentioned and meant to comfort, but it has been said, "The road to Hell is paved with good intentions." We got our fair share of pavement! But going through this with Macayla has made me realize I have poured some of that pavement for others as well. When we are on the outside looking in on someone's pain, it is hard to know what to say. It seems for many people it is even harder to say nothing at all. Silence does not appear to be an option, as it feels too awkward. It is understandable. However, we are not the only ones to experience this aspect of mourning. Job was also assaulted by faulty comfort from friends.

Job's life was in shambles. His wealth and family were decimated. His health ruined. Adorning torn garments he sat in ashes, scraping the puss-oozing sores on his body with pottery shards. Job's condition stirred others to respond. His wife was the one family member still alive and we have already heard her grief-stricken, bitter advice. Along came three friends who barely recognized Job. They were dismayed by his appearance and sat with him in silence for seven days. They saw his pain was great and said nothing. That is one of the best things we can do when we go to comfort those in pain. Often, a hurting person does not need words but just the presence of others. In fact, it may be the one in pain who needs to do the talking and do so without response or argument from us.

## We Weep With Those Who Weep: blog entry for May 27, 2009:

The past several weeks have been tough for several families we know. One family lost their child five days after birth. She was born at twenty-four weeks. Another family lost their daughter, age 19, after a stroke. She had spina bifida. Another family we know just delivered their full-term son only to find him without a heartbeat. He was revived and is in NICU now. Another family we know has a son with Battens and he was in the hospital for over a week and the doctors did not give him much chance of living. Fortunately, he is back home and doing well for now.

It is difficult to see all of this pain. It brings us closer to the reality of our own situation. We ache for these families and can relate to them, though we cannot know how they feel. Each of us goes through grief and suffering differently. What is shared are the tears. Jesus shared those tears at Lazarus' tomb. He wept for the grief death and sickness brings us. Further, God the Father is not aloof to our pain for He watched His only begotten

Son die on a cross. God the Father not only relates to how these parents feel, but He knows how they feel. He also has His arms around these children and nothing, not even death, can separate them from the love of God. Still, we ache and grieve, but not without hope.

All too often, we think we have to say just the right thing to a person in grief. Instead, we need to realize they may need to speak and what they say may be full of anger or even strange. Job spoke and cursed the day of his birth. He wished he had never been born, sparing him from these experiences. Job vented his lament, but upon hearing this, his friends could not keep their silence and felt compelled to respond. They wanted to "fix" things and this is not helpful for people in the throes of mourning. We cannot "fix" their grief. We cannot "fix" their situation. They may say something theologically unsound, but the last thing we need to be at that moment is the doctrine police. Our words will not magically make it all better or get them to "come around."

These friends claimed Job must have had some hidden sin, which brought about his calamity as punishment. Readers of the story are already aware Job was blameless and there was no sin for which he was struck. For the next twenty-eight chapters these friends continued to interrogate Job for his alleged, hidden sin but Job continued to declare his innocence. The text seems to drag on and on and, like Job, the reader gets frustrated with his friends. Job barked at his friends with sarcasm several times. "Truly then you are the people and with you wisdom will die!" (12:2) These friends attempt to demonstrate their wisdom as they describe God's justice and his punishment of wickedness. Logically this meant Job had sin in his life. Job responded to their *wisdom*, "Behold, my eye has seen all this, my ear has heard and understood it. What you know I also know; I am not inferior to you." In other words, Job was not stupid or ignorant of theology. Both he and his comforters claim they possess wisdom. Job chided, "You are worthless physicians…Your memorable sayings are proverbs of ashes, your defenses are defenses of clay." (13:1, 4, 12)

# WHAT NOT TO SAY

We can become worthless physicians to those in grief when we try to explain, fix or assuage their suffering. We think we are required to offer magical words of comfort, but we fumble and stumble because we have no idea what those words should be. Since our mourning started well before our daughter's funeral, many people attempted to make us feel better about the situation. We actually had a person say, "Jesus just needed another flower in his garden." My child is not a flower! Jesus did not come to earth and die on a cross to save flowers! My daughter is a human created in the image of God. Jesus even specifically clarified God's concern for us is greater than his concern for the "lilies of the field." (Matthew 6:28-30) When your child is dying, the last thing you want to hear is, "Look on the bright side, she'll be a plant in heaven!" Simplistic silver linings were of no help. This was one of the "proverbs of ashes" we heard in our grief.

Others wanted to defend God's honor as well. One person offered comfort stating, "God's plan is perfect." Another said, "God does not make mistakes." Well-intentioned people attempted to offer pithy theological statements to make us feel better. Theological platitudes, even true ones, are most often out of place during the storm of grief. Further, many times we twist the truth about God when we offer such statements out of context. One person may offer, "God's plan is perfect" to assert God's sovereignty while another offers, "This was a fluke of nature" absolving God of any responsibility. We forget God does not need our defense. In fact, we may push people away from him more by trying to explain everything in a short, pithy statement. "God does not make mistakes." While this is true, to one grieving, it can make God seem distant, capricious and cruel. How does this comfort? We cannot offer what God can. We cannot replace the council of God. So, we must be slow to offer cosmic-level reasons for someone's suffering. In our case, we wanted to know why this calamity has struck. We *demanded* to know why. We could only turn to God for such answers. Would he give us any answers and were we were ready for them?

# JOB WAS NOT INTO CLICHÉS

Job eventually demanded to know why God did these things to him. It is notable the text states Job did not sin with his first statements. In the beginning, he did not demand anything from God. After discovering his family and wealth were wiped out, Job stated, "Naked I came from my mother's womb, and naked I shall return there. The LORD gave and the LORD has taken away. Blessed be the name of the LORD" (Job 1:21) Over time the phrase, "The Lord giveth and the Lord taketh away" has become a cliché. Some use it as a dismissive c'est la vie. "Oh, well. Such is life. Let's move on." But that was not Job's attitude here. He was mourning. He was not dismissive or inattentive. He was hurting and sitting in ashes. The original audience would have gasped at this statement. The Hebrew word used in Job for "blessed" can also be translated as "cursed." This word choice keeps the audience on edge. Notice, Job also said, "The Lord gave and the Lord has taken away." He did not say Satan has taken anything away. The original audience would have seen this as borderline blasphemous. Thus, the author had to clarify for us in the very next sentence Job did not sin or blame God. In the beginning of the story, Job believes that God was still with him in the midst of the pain, but Job is not at peace.

In fact, God *was* with him. Thus, Satan complained after the first attack because Job failed to curse God. Satan's second attack comes after he complains Job is still too protected! He again asserts if the blessings of Job's personal health stop, Job will curse God. Imagine, Job has lost his children and fortune and Satan claims Job is still too blessed to curse God! So, Satan gained permission to attack Job's health. Once again, Job spoke in response to the new wave of misery, "'Shall we indeed accept good from God and not accept adversity?' In all this Job did not sin with his lips." (Job 2:10) Again, the poet of Job's story had to clarify that Job's statement was not sinful. But Job is not done. He did not make these statements as if they were clichés. He was not trying to simply appear strong in his suffering and keep up the appearance of a faithful believer. This is not simply lip service. Ancient audiences did not run the risk of perceiving these statements as clichés as we might today. In fact, Job comes very close to cursing God and this can keep the audience on edge. What is cliché to us was questionable theology to the original audience. When he curses the day of his birth, he is wishing God had not made him and that elicits a strong response from his friends because this comes even closer to cursing God.

## FROM GRIEF TO GOD

The wisdom of this story is found by contrasting the responses of Job's friends to the responses of God. On and on Job and his friends talked. Back and forth they debated and argued over Job's alleged sin and God's judgment. Everyone was responding to Job's insistence of his righteousness and then at the end of the story a fourth friend suddenly showed up and responded. Elihu is described as younger than everyone else in the story and for that reason he remained quiet during their speeches. But he was angered by Job's reliance on his own righteousness and the lack of a real response by the other friends. He could not keep quiet. He spoke and quoted many of the statements Job made to show where Job's perspective skewed. He rhetorically asked, "Why do you complain against Him that He does not give an account of all His doings?" (Job 33:13) Elihu is used in this story as a bridge between the counsel of men and the counsel of God. He is used to announce the coming of God who will be the last One to respond to Job's lament and subsequent skewed perspective.

Elihu also offers an anticlimactic, ironic and comical transition to break the tension of the long dispute that just took place. As many interpreters point out, Elihu is pedantic in his attempt to answer the problem of Job's suffering. He offers some theological truths, but his focus is not on Job's pain, just the talking points in Job's laments and speeches. Elihu is the young, "whipper-snapper," the doctrine police, who berates Job's friends for their poor arguments and Job for his insistence of righteousness, but not God's righteousness. It becomes comical as Elihu speaks of himself, "For I am full of words; the spirit within me constrains me. Behold, my belly is like unvented wine, like new wineskins it is about to burst. Let me speak that I may get relief; Let me open my lips and answer." (Job 32:18-20) Elihu basically refers to himself as full of hot air and wine! He is bloated to be sure.[xviii] But Elihu is not inserted into Job's poem just for laughs. He prepares the way for

God's speeches. Elihu's references to God as Creator transitions us into God's speech about the same. Elihu's speeches end as he compares God's presence to that of an ominous storm. Meanwhile, a storm is brewing in the background. Elihu is not the answer Job needs or is looking for, but he prepares us as an audience for the ultimate answer. God.

## GRIEF'S DISTORTION

In our grief, our perspective is certainly distorted and we can be led to false conclusions about God and ourselves. For some time after the diagnosis of our daughter, I demanded to know why. I wanted to get answers from God. I prayed and read Scripture. I cried and wept before God and all I heard was silence in return. Job experienced the same thing. He said, "I cry out to You for help, but You do not answer me; I stand up, and You turn Your attention against me." (Job 30:20) In the height of our grief, we are usually incapable of listening. I believe God does not answer our whys when we are demanding and shaking our fists at him. He knows we are not truly ready to listen and when we demand anything from God we are on dangerous ground. Our demands reveal that deep down we believe God is accountable to us and not the other way around. Job's first statements were not sinful because they never assumed God was accountable to him. However, as Job continued his lament and discourses, his perspective seemed to change. As is possible for anyone in pain, the more he thought about it, the angrier he became; the more betrayed he felt. Job repeatedly cited his righteousness and demanded God hear his case. Job's focus shifted more to his own righteousness than God's. This was Elihu's critique of Job and the same criticism applies to me.

Our pastor, Aaron Rayburn, preached a sermon on the "Lord's Prayer" in Matthew 6:5-15 and through this text exposed a real problem with our perspective and prayer concerning circumstances. Jesus not only gave the model prayer, he explained the difference between a faithful Christian prayer and a pagan prayer. In Matthew 6:5-9, Jesus gave examples of hypocrites and pagans praying. In both cases, these prayers approach God with a business-type of relationship. As long as we do all the religious stuff like go to church, tithe, pray the right words and formulas, God will answer our prayers. It is a performance-based relationship with God. But Jesus said we are to pray, "Our Father..." We are to approach God as a child approaches a father. This is a love-based relationship. When we pray like pagans and God does not grant us what we wish, we may respond with anger and believe God did not give us what we deserved. However, if we have not been fulfilling our religious obligations like tithing, going to church, etc. then we may believe God will not hear our prayer unless we do something "extra good." Essentially, we are looking to circumstances to gauge our relationship with God and when things are bad we can feel betrayed by God. When things are well, then it seems God is pleased with us.

Shortly after the diagnosis, I reminded God how "obedient" I was to his call on my life to go into ministry. I reminded God how "faithful" he was supposed to be. I reminded God of how often he had healed others and certainly he could do the same for my daughter. I reminded God of how many people would be impacted by such an irrefutable miracle. But God was silent. I operated under some false assumptions that God "faithfulness" made him accountable to me. Before I could hear God speak again, I had to be humbled. I had to be made aware of my false assumptions and expectations. I had to rediscover my relationship with God the Father was based on his love, not my performance. For Job, awareness was awakened by God's first speech. The friend, Elihu, prepared the way for God's speech. Elihu did not debate Job's outward obedience to God, but the attitude that had formed in the midst of his suffering. With that preparation in place, God spoke and broke the silence.

## THIS FAR, NO FARTHER

God's speeches are a long list of questions. This is frustrating after being bogged down for over thirty chapters of tedious debate. We want answers and all we get are questions. But God's speech to Job and his friends remind us of how small and uninformed we are. God did not speak out of a rainbow with gumdrops raining down on Job and layout all the answers as unicorns frolicked in the background. Instead, God spoke out a storm, a whirlwind, and asked rhetorical question after rhetorical question demonstrating how he created all things and holds them together. God's speech convicted Job of his declaration of things he did not know. Job repented. "He [Job] is beginning, not to solve the problem, but to rise above it. For the first time in the book he is taking his mind off himself, and putting it on the great Creator."[xix] God's second speech may seem a bit strange, but the references to the Leviathan and Behemoth should be seen as literary references to common myths of the ancient Middle East. They represent the forces of chaos that reigned before creation had order. Here God asserts that he is the one who brought order from chaos when he created everything.[xx] God is the Creator and nothing is beyond his power.

God then turned to Job's three friends and stated His anger with their counsel and their false testimony about God. Like Job, we can question if God really knows what he is doing. When we demand to know why suffering has come into our lives, we most often assume falsely we have enough wisdom to understand the answer. God's bombardment of questions at the end of the story demonstrates how we are often ill equipped to understand the deeper, cosmic reasons behind specific instances of suffering. When giving counsel to those in grief we must never try to explain or justify why suffering has come into their life. The most comforting words I heard after our daughter's diagnosis was from my friend, Charlie. He said, "This sucks. I love you." His words were direct, maybe crass to some, but extremely comforting. He acknowledged our hurt. His words did not try to explain away our pain or the circumstances. His words did not minimize. His words also affirmed he was present with us. By extension, God's presence could be felt through Charlie's willingness to come alongside.

Dr. George M. Schwab makes some extremely helpful conclusions from Job as it relates to sufferers and how we can counsel them. He gives three insights into counseling. First, sometimes there is no direct link between a person's personal sin and their suffering. My wife and I are both sinners, but God never revealed that our sin caused Macayla's disease. Second, "sufferers may never know why God has allowed destructive forces into their lives." Wisdom resides with God alone and human wisdom relies on fearing the Lord and departing from evil (Job 28:28). We are not equipped to truly and fully understand the cosmic reasons behind every situation. Third, "God governs even the tumultuous and chaotic aspects of life, even evil."[xxi] God limited how much Satan could do to Job. God's speeches demonstrated how He controls the most powerful forces in creation, even the chaos of the Behemoth and Leviathan. God sets limits on evil as he does the sea. "Thus far you shall come and no further." (Job 38:11) Macayla's disease progressed slower than it could have. Macayla's brother, Jacob, did not have Battens disease. For our family, God told Battens disease, "Thus far you shall come, but no farther."

Here is where many believers find comfort in Romans 8:28 acknowledging how God works all things together for the good of those who love him and are called according to his purpose. We can find comfort in the fact that God works all things to conform us to the image of Christ (Romans 8:29). We can know there is a bigger story behind it all and our lives are part of it. Our suffering is not wasted and neither are our blessings. Regardless if a life lasts only a few days like David's child or 140 years like Job, there is a purpose for it. We may not know all the reasons, but we can often see how it affects circumstances and motivations. We can watch how God works through them to weave the tapestry of redemptive history together.

Schwab also offers two things necessary for suffers that we see in Job's story: personal contact with God and complete restoration.[xxii] We have discovered the presence of God in multiple ways during our journey. We found His presence in times of prayer and the study of Scripture once we humbled ourselves and stopped demanding answers from God. We had to realize God owed us nothing but, in his graciousness, he was giving more answers and reassurance than we first realized. We discovered his presence in people like Charlie, our family and our church family. The Church is the "hands and feet of Christ" and through our fellow believers, we experienced the presence and comfort of God. We also experienced his presence by way of his provision to meet many of our needs. We experienced his presence within our family relationships as the four of us were drawn closer to him and one another. It was through this Presence we were able to come to peace about the fact Macayla would be healed. God eventually restored Job and she would be restored either with us or with Christ in heaven. We will see her whole again. Restoration is a promise we trust and in which we find strength and hope.

It is hard to imagine how Job could declare, "though He slay me, I will hope in Him." (13:15) In the midst of grief, we can find ourselves on a roller coaster of emotions and thought. One moment may be full of anger and the next laughter. We find moments where God's presence is overwhelming and others when he seems absent. This is why it is helpful to think through these things before calamity strikes. We can never be fully prepared for grief, but truth that has been digested and implanted in our hearts and minds offers comfort in moments of pain. This is not simply the abstract truth statements well intentioned people like Job's friends try to offer. We must dig into what Scripture reveals about a good God and suffering. When the grief comes, we will still struggle. We may even find ourselves like C.S. Lewis who said, "Meanwhile, where is God?... Not that I am (I think) in much danger of ceasing to believe in God. The real danger is of coming to believe such dreadful things about Him. The conclusion I dread is not, 'So there's no God after all,' but, 'So this is what God's really like. Deceive yourself no longer.'"[xxiii] Grief often obscures truth. In moments of clarity, we can remember the ultimate and full restoration that is promised, whether here on earth or in eternity with Christ.

## SELF-ASSESSMENT

1. When you or someone you know is suffering, what is your approach to comfort them?
2. If things go wrong in life, do you feel betrayed by God? Why?
3. How often do you feel like you are trying to earn God's love?
4. If Christ is in your life, how often does he sit on the throne of your heart? Just when things are bad? Good? Occasionally? Never?
5. Does the idea of God being sovereign bring you comfort, anger or confusion? Why? If someone were to comfort you in your circumstances, what would you want them to say?

# 7

# The Child Overcomes

*The Story of a Father and Son*

Prognosis and funeral are two terms that all too often go hand in hand. Prognosis comes from the Greek words *pro* meaning "prior" and *gnosis* meaning "knowledge." Prior knowledge is both a gift and a curse. We want to know what is coming, but then again ignorance can be bliss. During the time we searched for a diagnosis for our daughter, it was frustrating to not know the cause of her seizures and digression. When we finally had a diagnosis, it crushed us, but it also helped. We have watched other families go years without a diagnosis for their child's condition. The helplessness is overwhelming. There is the ever-present idea valuable time is being lost if the problem is treatable. Our diagnosis came relatively quick, around eight months, but it crushed the hope Macayla's health would improve. The diagnosis of Battens disease gave us prior knowledge of the blindness, wheelchairs, suction machines, and medications that were part of our family's future. It let us know a funeral was coming.

## THE AWKWARDNESS OF DEATH

Our first trip to the funeral home to preplan for Macayla was surreal. We went down into a basement to view caskets. Granted it was a nicely finished basement, but the profuse imagery in our culture's movies and television connecting death and basements made the experience disconcerting. The basement was a well-lit set of rooms, carpeted and clean, but I still knew we were in a basement. Our culture's media had tainted me. Furthermore, we were perusing caskets like we would vehicles at a car dealership. It is hard to know how to feel when trying to purchase a box in which to bury your daughter. The funeral home staff was wonderful and I do not envy their job. In spite of the "culture of death" found in our media, dealing with death in the real world has become an alien process in our culture and by extension so has the funeral. We avoid pain and discomfort to the degree death is no longer thought of as a normal part of life. Most Americans do not like the idea of prearranging our funerals. It feels weird, scary and morbid.

The process is bizarre but it allows for the whole spectrum of emotions. During the process there were moments of love, grief, pain, laughter, joy, nostalgia, and hope. We found ways to joke and reminisce. Macayla always loved butterflies and we discussed the possibility of releasing them at the cemetery. They represent transformation as the caterpillar "dies" a worm and is reborn a butterfly. However, I always said Macayla liked horses better. For some reason, they could not release a herd of horses in the cemetery. In those moments, we also found our weakness could highlight the strength of Christ. It is difficult to make these decisions ahead of time because we would have rather focused on our daughter's life in the present and not think of her being gone in the future. But we chose to make those decisions beforehand so we would not have to wade through them in a fog of grief the day after Macayla's death. We were only able to do this through the grace and strength of our Lord.

The receiving of friends before a funeral has a whole mix of emotions. Usually the casket is open for viewing. People file by in line, view the body, greet the family and move on back to their lives, or anticipate the funeral. The people in line are nervous, as they are not sure what to say. The normal greetings we use in our culture suddenly become awkward. "Good to see you," seems out of place. "How are you?" becomes an insult. The meaning of our little etiquettes suddenly come under scrutiny and we are left tongue-tied. But remaining silent seems unbearable. What are we to say? Viewing the body also carries a mixture of feelings for many people. For those who did not know the deceased very well, the body can seem alien or even frightening. For those who knew the deceased well, the lifeless body can make their loved one seem unfamiliar. Then there is the comment, "Oh, he looks so good," or "Oh, she is just beautiful!" But that is not an honest, objective assessment. In spite of a mortician's best effort, a corpse is still a corpse. The lifeless shell is not beautiful. But what else should we say? Should we stare? Should we look away? We do not want to appear insensitive to the family's loss by averting our sight or staring, but most of us do not see a dead body everyday. For those in the line, there can be a mixture of fear, morbid curiosity, and awkwardness. But ultimately love and compassion can trump this mixture of sentiments and drive people to wait in this line.

The receiving family is exhausted. Even with planned funerals, there are many details the family must work out between the time of death and the funeral service. Often their exhaustion is only outmatched by their numbness. The mind is not as sharp as usual. Who did you talk to? Did everyone who needed to know of the death get the word? Were all the final details worked out? Standing in a line talking to many people, some familiar and some not as familiar, becomes a blur. Faces become smudged in the memory and words are vague. Unfortunately the family hears many of the theological or greeting-card clichés repeated. But there is something powerful about this portion of a funeral. As the one left behind to receive these folks, your emotions can swing wildly or go numb. Depending on the relationship, your reaction and emotions vary with each person offering condolences. It can be powerful to hear from a stranger how our loved one impacted their life. But when it is all said and done, regardless of the emotional disarray of the moment, the memory of being surrounded by family and friends at such a moment brings comfort. The funeral process may seem futile at the time, but one of the strongest memories that will remain is the presence of others. It does not even have to be the memory of specific people, but just the memory of others being with you. The hugs, handshakes and tears most often last longer than the words and, thankfully, even the poorly chosen words.

## THE PAIN OF DEATH

Jesus went to the funeral of his friend Lazarus (John 11). Jesus could have healed Lazarus the moment he became ill, but purposefully did not. Jesus could have shown up before they prepared Lazarus' body for burial and raised him from the dead, but he did not. This is why Mary and Martha, Lazarus' sisters, were so upset when Jesus showed up "late." Why did he not do something? Jesus came four days after the death while the mourners still wailed and the tears still fell, but he came with the intent of raising Lazarus from the dead. Jesus knew Lazarus would live again. Jesus knew he would go to the tomb and call Lazarus out. But when he came and saw the people mourning, Jesus wept. Jesus did not weep for the loss of Lazarus as much as the pain and grief death causes. He wept because his original creation was not intended to be this way. If only humanity had chosen love and not selfishness, death would have never entered the world (Genesis 3). Jesus wept for the mourners. Jesus wept for his children and creation that has been hurt so deeply by sin and death. The God of the universe wept for us. This is not a God in the palatial courts of heaven aloof to our suffering. This is the God of the universe who understands our suffering better than we do. He has walked in our shoes and he has felt our pain. Our pain pains him.

The story of a special father-son relationship demonstrates this truth beautifully. This son, like our daughter, had a prognosis of immanent death. The end would not be a gentle passing either, but horribly painful. The son was distressed as he was fully aware of what was coming. He hoped for a last minute miracle. He hoped he could somehow not go through it, but he also knew the reality of his life and his death. It was coming. What made this even more difficult was the fact he and his father had always been inseparable. They went everywhere together. He asked his father if there were any other way. "No," his father said, "there is no other way this can happen." Soon, death would separate them. So, the son spent a lot of time with his father, mother and friends. His father comforted him as long as possible, but when the pain started his friends abandoned him. His father stayed with him even when his mother could not. But at the very end, the father even turned his back on him and left. The son felt more than the physical pain racking his body. He felt the loneliness of death. He was cutoff.

Why would this father, so closely knit to his son, suddenly abandon him at the end? The son asked the same question in his native tongue, "Eli, Eli, lama sabachthani?" or "My God, My God why have You forsaken me?" (Matt 27:46) God the Father forsook Jesus on a cross in first century Palestine. His mother, Mary stood below, watching. She may have been only a few yards away, but she might as well have been on the other side of the universe. She could not take on his pain for him. She could not take his place on the cross, though she might have wanted to try. Instead, he was taking her place on the cross. He was taking our place on the cross. He who knew no sin, became sin on our behalf. This is where this Father and Son had to part ways. The Son took the just wrath our sin deserves.

How does this beautifully demonstrate God understands our pain? As the father of a dying child, I know God the Father has also lost his child. I also know God the Son experienced loss and grief from a human perspective when he became flesh and walked the earth. Jesus knows what it is like to suffer on a human level. He knows it more deeply than we will ever know. God is transcendent, but he has chosen to be immanent with us by working through and in our lives. God became flesh and dwelt among us in the first century. Jesus is the mediator between God and us and for that reason he is referred to as a "high priest" (Hebrews 4-7). Because he was here in the flesh and went through the same human experience we do, we discover he is a present help for us as well. "For we do not have a high priest who cannot sympathize with our weaknesses, but One who has been tempted in all things as we are, yet without sin. Therefore, let us draw near with confidence to the throne of grace, so that we may receive mercy and find grace to help in time of need." (Hebrews 4:15-16) Even though he has gone back to heaven, his Spirit is still a present help today for those of us who belong to him. God the Spirit dwells in believers. God the Father calls us to him. God the Son provides the way to him. Through it all, God still dwells among his people, providing his mercy and grace in our time of need.

## GOD'S RELATIONSHIPS

This may seem confusing if we are not familiar with what is referred to as the Trinity. Christians believe in one God. One Being, sovereign and all-powerful. Christianity teaches God revealed himself in Scripture and history in such a way as we are left with this conclusion about him: God is one Being, but three Persons. It is like the fact I am known as Jeff. However, as Jeff I am a father, a son, and a husband. I am three "persons" but one creature. Now, these "persons" actually describe how I relate to others outside of myself. But God's three persons describe how he relates *within* himself. God the Father is always a father to God the Son. God the Son is always a son to the Father. God the Spirit is always the Spirit going forth from the Father and Son. They are not three different ways God manifests himself at different times. When Jesus was baptized, God the Son was in the water, God the Father spoke from heaven and God the Spirit showed up as a dove simultaneously (Matthew 3:16-17). All three Persons of the Trinity are equally God. They do not divide God up into three slices. They are distinct persons, but unified in one Being. Yes, it is hard for our minds to fully understand, but this is what Scripture affirms. This is not what we would expect if Christianity were purely an invention of humans. The first Christians were Jews and firmly monotheistic. It would have been easier to avoid this triune description, but apparently they were convinced God revealed himself in this way and they wrote it down in what we now call Scripture. Some may claim Christianity was a synthesis of Judaism and the polytheism of Greco-Roman culture, however the New Testament writings refute this and affirm a monotheistic perspective (John 1; Acts 17; James 2:19). Though it is hard to grasp, there are still many aspects of God that make sense if the Trinity is true. The most obvious is that of relationships.

The God of the universe could have designed all of existence in multiple ways or not at all, but he designed it in a way that reflects him. God created everything in relationships. The days of creation in Genesis are not isolated events. Each day relates to the others. The light created on the first day relates to the stars, moon, and sun created on the fourth day. The vegetation created on the third day used this same light. Humans, created on the sixth day, utilize the light to see and mark the passage of time. Creation was not complete until all of its relationships were established. Genesis does not go into precise and protracted detail about the process, but it certainly demonstrates the relational pattern found in creation. Humans were also created in relational terms and were intended to relate to God. With each day of creation, God saw what he made "was good." It was not until the sixth day, when all of the relationships were in place and creation was complete, God said, "It is very good." The Triune God relates within himself as Father and Son and Spirit and this relational attribute undergirds all of creation.

With the introduction of sin and death, this reflection was marred and relationships broke down. What was "very good" became corrupt. Again, God had options for how he could have dealt with this, including the destruction of everything and starting over. Instead, he held it together and revealed himself directly to humanity through Scripture. He inspired multiple people over many centuries to write about the circumstances and events in which they found themselves. He inspired them to do more than simply write down brute facts. He inspired them to write a theological history, meaning they reported how God was involved in these events. I could tell Macayla's story and simply report her medical history and it would sound like a medical case study. On the other hand, I could tell of her medical history and how God worked through it. This is Macayla's "theological history," though it is not inspired or inerrant.

## GOD'S FLESH

God inspired the Old Testament authors to prepare humanity for the day he would put on flesh and dwell among us. Then God worked through a few more authors to report this incarnation and its consequences in theological and redemptive history. We call this the New Testament. Included in the New Testament is a record of God speaking to a young girl in first century Nazareth. He told her his Spirit would come upon her and cause a pregnancy. This child was a result of God's Spirit and Mary's egg. This is not to say Jesus was a mixture of God and man. Jesus was completely God and completely man. In spite of this mathematical impossibility, Jesus was in fact God in the flesh. He had the divine will and a human will. When he spoke of God, he spoke of God as his Father. When God spoke of Jesus during the baptism in the Jordan, God referred to Jesus as his Son. They were not speaking of each other in generic terms, but according to the eternal relationship that exists between them. It is this relationship God would use to redeem all of the other relationships sin and death had disrupted.

Jesus, God the Son, is of the same substance as God the Father. This is why Jesus referred to himself as the "only begotten Son of God." The word "begotten" means to be made of the same "stuff." We can carve statues representative of humans, but our begotten children are actually human. Jesus is not merely representative of God, but he is God. When Christians refer to themselves as children of God, they mean "adopted" children and not "begotten." We are not the same substance as God. God the Son had to become flesh if redemption would ever truly be realized for humanity and creation. God is just and holy. When sin entered, his creation became unholy and justice had to be carried out. Instead of carrying it out on us, God became flesh and took it upon himself at the cross.

As stated earlier, crime creates a debt to society. Likewise, sin creates a debt with God. Anselm of Canterbury was a bishop and theologian around the turn of the twelfth century who provided a helpful explanation for why Jesus had to be fully God while being fully man. He essentially said our sin dishonors the holiness of God and creates this "debt." Dishonoring the infinite God creates an infinite debt. But humans are limited, finite. Being finite, we are incapable of paying an infinite debt. The only being capable of paying an infinite debt is the infinite God, but he does not owe the debt, we do. In other words, we owe a debt we cannot pay. God is the only one who can pay the debt, but he does not owe it. However, God loves us so much, he became flesh in Jesus Christ so being man he was in the proper position to pay the debt and being God he was capable of paying the debt.[xxiv] Further, we must understand Jesus' human will always submitted to his divine will. We only have a human will, but we struggle to submit to God's will and fail to do so daily. The other word for this lack of submission is called sin. Unlike us, Jesus' human will always submitted, thus he was sinless. Being a truly sinless human and God, he was the only one capable to die for the sins of others.

## MORE THAN WE CAN BEAR

What does all this theology tell us? Foremost, it tells us God is not arbitrary or disconnected from us, but in fact wants us to be connected to him. We must remember David's child also belonged to God even though he struck him. Further, we must remember God struck his Child as well when God the Father forsook God the

Son on the cross. It is amazing to think how the sin problem that disrupted the relationships within creation as well as between creation and Creator was reconciled by God disrupting the relationship within himself. He has reconciled the world to himself in Christ and offers reconciliation to us. (2 Corinthians 5:16-21) "He made Him who knew no sin to be sin on our behalf, so that we might become the righteousness of God in Him." (v. 21)

"My God, My God, why have You forsaken Me?" the Son cried out from the cross. This was not a question merely cried out in the pain of separation, but it also is the first line of what we call Psalm 22. Some of the Jews standing near the cross misunderstood Jesus words and thought he was calling for Elijah. (Matt 27:47) But obviously, some heard and understood what was said. The Jews standing near the cross that understood Jesus' cry would have recognized it as Psalm 22. They would have realized how it foretold of the very scene unfolding before their eyes. They would see the pierced hands and feet the psalm spoke of centuries before Roman crosses were put to use. They would have seen Jesus' garments being divided among the Roman soldiers casting lots as promised in this psalm one thousand years earlier. Maybe they remembered Psalm 22 also foretold how this reconciliation would be pronounced to all nations and future generations. This was not merely an exercise of justice and punishment. It was prophesy fulfilled. It was the bridging of the infinite chasm between God and man. It was redemption.

God has not abandoned us to destroy ourselves or be destroyed by his justice. He forsook the Son at the cross instead of forsaking us. He is concerned about our lives, even the life of a child like Macayla. Of course, we would prefer God show his concern by simply fixing Macayla's brain and genes so she could live life like the rest of us. But even if he did heal her of Battens, she would eventually face death again just as Jesus' friend Lazarus. We often forget Lazarus had to die twice and people mourned him twice. I would imagine the second funeral had a hope the first one lacked. If God healed Macayla of Battens and she lived, would he heal her later when death revisits? What if she has cancer at age forty-eight? What if she has a stroke at age seventy-eight? When would it end? God will intervene sometimes and treat the symptoms of a fallen world, but what he did on the cross and at the tomb did not just treat symptoms of a fallen world, it cured the disease.

Just before his arrest, Jesus told his disciples he would be leaving soon. His discourse is recorded for us in John 14-17. He was not speaking of the crucifixion, but of his ascension into heaven after the resurrection. The Son would go back to the Father. Jesus did not have to tell his friends this. He did not have to say anything about anything. But he did because he cared for them and he cares for us. Thus, he explained to his friends God the Spirit would come after the ascension to guide, teach and help create the Scriptures of the New Testament (John 16:12-14). God did not have to inform us about anything, but he did because we are not abandoned. We may not have the answers to every question, but we have the answers we need. In fact, Jesus said he had so much more he wanted to say, but he did not because the disciples could "not bear it." (John 16:12) Jesus wanted to prepare them for what was coming, but neither they nor us can bear to know all that will happen.

It is the prognosis, the foreknowledge, we cannot bear because it involves suffering in the early stages. Jesus, God's only begotten Son, would be abandoned at the cross and he knew it. He even told his disciples this portion of the prognosis. He said, "Behold, an hour is coming, and has already come, for you to be scattered, each to his own home, and to leave Me alone; and yet I am not alone, because the Father is with Me." (John 16:32) Jesus knew the disciples would run when the angry mob came and arrested him. When his friends abandoned him, the Father stayed with the Son. Jesus knew they would experience fear, doubt and guilt. He wanted to tell them more so maybe they would understand as the events unfolded, but they "could not bear it."

It is amazing to think how much Jesus had to bear at the cross. He knew every person he was redeeming through his actions there. He knew every sin he was dying for and by whom it was committed. He knew the separation he would experience there, separation from his friends, his mother, and eventually from the Father. "My God, My God, why have You forsaken me?" But he also knew the joy enduring the cross would eventually bring (Hebrews 12:2). Jesus knows more than we can imagine or bear. This is why he alone is the "author and perfecter of faith." He knows faith is what we need to bear this fallen world.

## HOW WE LIVE THROUGH IT

Having faith does not exempt a person from hardship and in fact can bring about more suffering. The author of Hebrews defines faith as "the assurance of things hoped for, the conviction of things not seen" (Hebrews 11:1). It is assurance and conviction, not wishful thinking. Then the author goes on to list multiple people of faith in Scripture ranging from Abel to the prophets. He wrote of how many of these people were able to perform miracles and turn back armies through faith. But the list of accomplishments flows right into a list of sufferings, torture, and death these faithful people of God experienced. Would these people have followed God if they knew beforehand death and pain was part of the plan? Would we? The fact is we know we will suffer in this world. But if we know Christ, if we are assured and convicted of what he did for us at the cross, then there is a joy set before us as well. There is an ultimate joy included in our prognosis. It is this joy of Christ that makes our sufferings more bearable.

Christianity is not wishful thinking. When Christians speak of hope and faith, they speak of assurance and conviction. I have a friend who said he did not believe in Hell, or Heaven for that matter because if we get so focused on the afterlife we will not be much good here and now. He also stated we create our own heaven and hell here on earth. My friend also wears the label "Christian" by the way. Unfortunately, this misunderstanding of Heaven and Hell is prevalent. The concepts of Heaven and Hell are not a made-up doctrines used to keep people in line by threatening unwanted behavior with a promise of Hell and good behavior with the promise of Heaven. I do not deny people have had the Hell literally scared out of them such as the case of the sailors with Jonah. However, Heaven and Hell are part of reality and if we ignore their existence, our lives here and now will be lived in delusion. Christians are not meant to use Heaven as an excuse to daydream their way through life with visions of better times ahead. We were meant to take life head-on knowing there is an ultimate resolution to all things. There is an ultimate joy through which we live life here and now. That joy enables us to do so because its source is Christ who is bigger than the here and now. We have been supported through our loss by the joy and promise of Christ. Heaven has not distracted us, but motivated us to be more active in the here and now.

Some skeptics think the worst insult they can throw at Christians is that we use God as a crutch. They are right, but they only insult themselves. Everyone needs a "crutch." True Christ followers are at least intelligent and honest enough to recognize and admit it. If we could correct all of our problems on our own power, we would have done it already. Humans are obviously unable to truly fix themselves. This insult may also assume there is nothing beyond the here and now of life on earth. However, Christ followers are aware of reality and more accurately than atheists. We know there is life beyond what we experience here. We know there is a bigger picture to reality even though our eyes may not see it as clearly as we would like. It is the atheists who live in denial and delusion. In a situation like Macayla's, the atheist is left to the pain and misery of hopelessness. They have to turn to distractions for their crutch. Vacations, television, substance abuse or any other form of distraction can become the crutch used to cope with tragedy. This is not to claim all distractions are bad. Vacations or just sitting through a movie to take a break from it all can be therapeutic. But these distractions do not have to be the "crutch" for Christians.

Another tactic I have seen used by parents of dying children is denial. They simply ignore the prognosis and focus only on the "happy" moments. But Christ calls us to follow him by taking up our cross daily. He calls us to follow him through the valley of the shadow of death, not in denial, not in distraction, but in full acknowledgment and trust. We are to follow the Shepherd. The joy of the greener pastures and still waters is before us, but the trail leading there is dark and at times dangerous. We are not meant to walk that trail with our eyes closed. Yes, we who believe have a crutch because we know the reality of our situations. We know we need it. Denial of our present circumstances or the ultimate reality of Heaven and Hell is neither healthy nor sane.

We had the prognosis for Macayla just as David had the prognosis for his unnamed child. We knew death was immanent. We knew there was no human intervention that could stop it. All we could do was rely on Christ. David turned to God, fasting and praying. This should not be seen as simply sitting in idle, wishful thinking. David utilized the options he had. We turned to God as well, praying, fasting, anointing, medicating, and intervening where we could to make her more comfortable. But that's all we could do. The rest was up to God. But will God handle the "rest" the way we want? Before we can know the answer to this question, we must ask ourselves if what we want is truly the best thing. By "best" I mean best for us, our loved ones, humanity, creation and all of history in light of God's desire for redemption. We are incapable of planning on such a scale. We are incapable of knowing what is best in the true and whole sense of the term. Once we recognize this reality, once we clearly see the prognosis, then we can be more effective in living in the here-and-now. Only then can we, through prayer and supplication with much thanksgiving, know the best decisions to make. We are able to hear our Shepherd's voice and follow Him down the "best" path, though it be dark and treacherous at times.

The special relationship between the Father, Son and Spirit gives us the foundation for creation and our re-creation. Through a relationship with Christ, we are transformed and freed from the awkwardness of death. We have a new prognosis. In Christ, we may walk through the valley of the shadow of death, but not death itself, just the shadow. We will suffer in this world, and sometimes more because of our faith, but we know there is an ultimate joy set before us. The Son assumed our frailty and faced our pain and temptation. We are not left to ourselves to worship an aloof God somewhere, up there. We have access to the very throne of God. Finally, because of this relationship, our other relationship with others can begin to take their proper shape.

## SELF-ASSESSMENT

1. Have you taken the cross for granted in your struggles? Can you see how God becoming flesh and dying on the cross would put all of your circumstances into a new perspective?
2. What is your understanding of "faith?"
3. How does your faith inform you concerning your circumstances?
4. What is your impression of Heaven and Hell? Who goes there? What difference does this prior knowledge make in daily life?

5. Does the idea of following Christ in the midst of your circumstances make you feel angry, betrayed, inconvenienced, or delighted? Why?
6. Read Matthew 27-28 and Psalm 22 in the same sitting. Can you see the crucifixion described in Psalm 22? Don't miss the end of that Psalm! Did the things it describes come to pass?

# 8

# The Lord Saved the Child

*The Story of Macayla's Healing*

I pushed Macayla in her wheelchair to the checkout at the pet store and placed the chew toy on the counter. The nice woman behind the counter looked at Macayla and asked, "Oh, is this for your dog?" It was the only time I was thankful Macayla could not talk! Macayla had reached a point in her digression where she began chewing on everything. It is a common symptom among children with neurological damage. Because she was older and stronger, she easily ripped baby chew toys and that presented a choking hazard. In search of a solution, I took Macayla to the pet store and shopped for chew toys. It sounds bad to those who have never faced this, but it is really the only way to protect a child who is compulsively chewing and is too strong for baby toys. We found a blue, rubber toy, which was easy for her to hold, would not tear and she could not choke on it. When we got to the checkout and the lady asked the question, what was I supposed to say? What would this woman think? Would she call child-protective services? I struggled with how to respond and basically said, "Sorry, Macayla is unable to speak in full sentences."

I regret not taking the time to explain our situation. We have found such moments to be opportunities that open the door to meaningful discussions to share the love of Christ. My wife has always been better with sharing in everyday conversation than me. The chew toy was one of the special memories I had with Macayla. It may seem silly, but I found there have been so many little moments etched into my memory while other "big" moments have faded. We discovered memories could offer either pain or comfort. Some make us smile and others make us ache.

However, I think some people were perplexed at the visitation prior to Macayla's funeral. Some people struggled to understand how we were not crying as much as they were. Unfortunately, this may have given the wrong impression of our faith and we could not communicate with everyone why our tears did not flow as quickly as theirs. My concern was people would misunderstand the lack of tears at the visitation as denial driven by religion. But we in fact had shed many tears prior to her death. We started grieving four and a half years prior to her funeral. We sobbed many times as we watched our little girl lose more and more of her abilities. I had prayed so many times for a different prognosis. I grieved for the steady stream of losses throughout Macayla's life and for the loss of future possibilities. Macayla and we grieved as she lost the ability to coordinate her hands to grab toys she wanted. I can still remember her inconsolable crying at bath time when she was no longer able to pour water from one cup to another, as this was a favorite activity for her. I grieved over her loss of teen years, which may sound crazy to those who presently have teenagers. I grieved over the loss of giving her away at a wedding. I grieved over the loss of possible grandchildren through our daughter. By the time the funeral came, our family was at a different stage of grief than our fellow mourners, but our tears were not finished.

## GIVING HER AWAY

The story of Macayla takes us to a funeral and a wedding. It takes us where we never wanted to go, had it been our decision, but it is a place of healing. The day my little girl was born, I thought of my role as a father. I had to protect her. I wanted to keep her from dating as long as possible since I am all too familiar with the mindset of boys. I wanted to prepare her by taking her on dates with me first and demonstrating what kind of treatment she should expect from boys. They should open her door, treat her with honor and keep her safe. Maybe if I set the bar high enough she would have never dated, as no boy could live up to her expectations! I wanted to help her shop for bathing suits each summer and help her understand how modesty can be attractive. This would have been vital since we discovered later how much Macayla loved the beach and swimming. I looked forward and saw a day I may have to give her to a young man in marriage. I would walk her down the aisle and on behalf of her mother and me, I would give over the role I had played to another man. He would protect her, provide for her and become the number one man in her life. When I saw my infant daughter in the hospital for the first time, I never imagined I would walk her down the aisle nine years later and she would be in a casket.

Death has been portrayed in poetic and even romantic terms, but dying is atrocious. There is nothing beautiful about watching someone die. There is nothing poetic about someone's body struggling to live. It is a horrible sight. We watched our daughter die slowly. Her last week of life was the hardest as her body shut down. Kidney function ceased, causing other areas of her body to swell with fluids. Stool backed up into the stomach and leaked out around her feeding tube. Her lungs gurgled with every breath as they filled with fluids. Her skin began to change color as the circulation centralized to the torso. Her once soft, peach skin became mottled with blue and gray splotches. Her lips turned deep purple. Her tongue swelled. There was nothing beautiful about it. Even after she died, her corpse looked yellowish-white. It was not my little girl that lay in the bed. It was a shell. During my short time in law enforcement, I had seen dead bodies in wrecks and crime scenes, some with horrific injuries. But my daughter's body was the most difficult to view. It was the most horrifying even though there were no external injuries. Dying is horrendous enough to make death a preferred, even beautiful, option.

We knew the prognosis of death for Macayla. We knew unless God miraculously rebuilt her brain and reengineered her genes, she would die. We also had a prognosis about death itself. Paul wrote to believers in Thessalonica, "But we do not want you to be uniformed, brethren, about those who are asleep, so that you will not grieve as do the rest who have no hope. For if we believe that Jesus died and rose again, even so God will bring with Him those who have fallen asleep in Jesus." (1 Thessalonians 4:13-14) But prior knowledge is not the same as experience.

I struggled here differently than my wife during the last week of Macayla's life. I knew Macayla was at the end, but I could not honestly pray for her to go ahead and die. I knew if she died she would be in heaven and be healed. I knew if she died there would be no more Battens disease. In spite of this prior knowledge, I could not pray for death to come. I told her repeatedly she could go home when she was ready and we would be o.k. This is the only time I lied to my daughter. I said this for her benefit, but I did not mean it. In spite of the prior knowledge and preparation for her death, in spite of the atrocious effects dying was having on her little body, I selfishly wanted her to stay. I could not pray for God to help her leave until the last day.

## WITH HOPE

The last day of Macayla's life was her ninth birthday. We celebrated with decorations and birthday cake. We even had a lot of family around for the last two days of her life here on earth. It was good for all of us in many respects. For those who had not been able to be around Macayla on a daily basis and had never seen anyone die, it gave them time to adjust. It helped everyone get over the shock of being in a room with a *dying* person and settle down next to *the person*. She was not a dying Macayla, just Macayla. It took me those few days to reach a point that I could honestly let go. I am so thankful for that time, as hard as it was, since most situations do not afford such an opportunity. Often the death of a loved one comes so sudden there is no opportunity to prepare, much less come to any kind of peaceful release. That release usually comes much later for the mourner, if at all. What helped me let go was a song by Steven Curtis Chapman I had used in a video. Two weeks prior to Macayla's death, I put together a video slideshow of photos for the funeral. I did not want to have to scramble at the last minute to put one together. Since one of my hobbies is videography and photography, I wanted to put this video together myself. It was one of my ways to be "prepared."

The background music for this video included Steven's song *With Hope*. The song reflects what Paul wrote to the Thessalonians:

> And we can grieve with hope,
> 'Cause we believe with hope
> There's a place by God's grace

> Where we'll see your face, again.
> We'll see your face again.
>
> So we can cry with hope,
> And say goodbye with hope.
>
> We wait with hope
> And we ache with hope.
> We hold on with hope.
> We let go with hope.[xxv]

God's word does not declare Christians are exempt from grief. Thessalonians 4:13 does not say Christians will not grieve. The verse says, "…so that you will not grieve AS DO THE REST who have no hope." We most certainly grieve, but we grieve with hope. This hope does not remove or neutralize the grief. It gives us strength to wade through it. Christians do not mourn less than non-Christians. In fact Jesus mourned (John 11). We grieve with a bigger perspective. Late in the afternoon, about seven hours before Macayla died, I watched the video I made and heard Chapman's song. It helped me have a cathartic burst of emotion. It helped me let go. It helped me remember that I grieve, but not in the same way others without Christ grieve. I was finally at a new level of peace about Macayla's full healing in heaven. I was ready to walk her down the aisle.

Throughout the Bible, marriage is one of the metaphors for the relationship God has with his people. Like marriage, it is meant to be exclusive, faithful, intimate and above all other relationships. In the New Testament, believers in Christ are part of the Church and the Church is the "bride" of Christ. It is through this truth I was able to see Macayla's funeral was in some ways like a wedding. We walked her down the aisle and gave her away to the Groom of grooms. Macayla's funeral was not a grueling solemnization of death and separation. It was a celebration of her life here and her union with Christ. It was a moment to remember where she had been and celebrate where she is now. It was an opportunity to worship the God who made her healing possible for he is the Author of life and the Giver of hope. There is no one more qualified to care for my daughter than Christ. When I walked my daughter down the aisle and gave her away, I gave my role of protector and provider to another Man, the God-Man, Jesus. Macayla traded up.

## WITHOUT MEDICATION

I certainly had hope and a peace I never experienced to such a degree before. However, I still only had a few, sparse tears. I know every person grieves differently, but I needed to cry and could not. This is where taking an antidepressant can certainly hinder the natural process of grieving. There were these surreal moments after Macayla went home where I found myself crying without tears. I felt as if I was crying but no tears flowed. Other times I would actually start crying only to have it dry up before I was finished. It is strange and difficult to understand why drops of salty water coming from our eyes is important, but without them, my grieving was hindered. The danger of antidepressants is that we can take them to help us function through depression but never actually deal with the issues. That is why I regret not seeking counsel before starting the medication. The medication certainly helped me function, but it kept me from grieving fully when the time came. Once I realized this, I weaned off the medication. I needed to go through the full process of grief. Otherwise, Macayla would be the only one who found healing in all of this.

I also discovered how taking an antidepressant for two years stunted my growth in Christ. As soon as I weaned off the drug, I found I was able to cry again. In fact, the week I started weaning off the medication, I cried in Macayla's bed for almost an hour one night. I found I was able to appropriately tear up and cry at other moments. But I also found my anger flared to heights it had not in over two years. I found myself struggling with lust in a way I had not in two years. My emotional response to situations became less mature than they had been while on the medication. The medication had dampened my emotional responses to situations, but I had erroneously assumed this dampening was a sign of maturity. When we cannot experience our emotional responses properly, we are not aware of the problem in our character and thinking. I view emotions much like nerves in the nervous system. When I touch something hot, the nerves in my fingers send a signal to my brain to pull away. It protects my body. Then I can assess what this hot item was and learn to avoid this danger in the future. I think emotions can function in a similar capacity. When I have an emotional response to a situation, it should alert me to think, not feel, my way through the situation. It should immediately make me assess why I am reacting in a particular way. Often we allow our emotional responses to get the best of us and we turn to coping mechanisms. Instead, we must turn to the truth and grace of Christ to assess our character and response. Grace and truth are not coping mechanisms, but *character-changing* mechanisms.

Once the medication was removed, I discovered there were several struggles that needed to be addressed. The antidepressant prevented me from recognizing my need to deal with these problems before. My body also revolted and had mild withdrawals. I stopped the medication slowly and under a doctor's supervision, but it was not comfortable or pleasant. Some days I felt as though I were dizzy or drunk. This brought on the temptation to just start taking the medicine again to stop this feeling. Again, it is sometimes easier to take a pill than to trust that God and his word are sufficient. Some will object and say that depression is a chemical imbalance in the brain and to make people believe they can overcome it through faith is tantamount to telling cancer patients to not seek medical treatment. This is not what I am saying or advocating. In our culture we believe life is only good when we are "happy." When we are unable to be happy, we want someone to fix it. Certainly there are folks who have some deep-rooted issues, possibly brain malfunctions that may require medication to help. However, there are many people like me who simply confuse natural, emotional conditions such as grief with depression. There are many people on antidepressants like me who do not have a full-fledged chemical imbalance in their brain that requires medication. Grief hurts physically, emotionally, and mentally. It is part of life. All I advocate is that a person make a truly informed decision through both biblical counseling and their medical doctor. This way, all the bases are covered.

I came off the medication and Jennifer and I sought counseling. It helped me to release emotions and confess where I was still struggling. I found myself wanting Macayla back. I wanted her back so much I would have taken her just as she was, Battens and all. But this was selfish and wrong, not that she could actually come back, short of a miracle. It was an indicator of a potential stumbling block in my thinking and relationship with God. Macayla was healed. She was in the best place she could be but I wanted her back even though it would put her in the pain and loss of this world with me. It is completely understandable to want the ones we lose to be back with us. However, we must allow that desire, as with all desires, to be tempered by God. This understandable desire can metamorphose into an idol. It can become a wedge in our relationship with God. This desire can become bitterness toward God and skew our perspective. What starts as a natural and understandable wish can become a destructive and delusional desire.

One remarkable phrase stuck in my mind during this time and helped me with the withdrawals of the medication and the increase in emotions. In counseling with our pastor and friend he stated that as I came off of these medications I might discover it was God's will for me to feel bad. What?! God may actually want us to feel bad? As crazy as this sounds to most of us, there is a time and place in each of our lives where this is true. Paul wrote to the Corinthians and spoke of a "thorn in his flesh" that he asked three times for God to remove. Now here is Paul THE Apostle praying faithfully for God to heal whatever this problem was, be it medical or relational, and God said, "No." There are times when God will not heal or fix our problems and instead give us the same answer he gave Paul. "My grace is sufficient for you, for power is perfected in weakness." (See 2 Corinthians 12) It was God's will for Paul to continue in this problem. It was not God's will for Paul to feel good or be "happy" in this situation. There are times when it is God's will for us to feel bad and struggle so that God's strength and power are unmistakable in our lives.

Macayla's Grace: blog for February 14, 2010

I sat down to update this blog and was

about to write how Macayla seems to have finally found some rest after staying awake most of the night. I was about to write how she finally sounded like she was breathing fine and didn't need suctioning for the thousandth time. I was about to write about how peaceful she looks. But she came out of sleep to cough and sputter once again. I just wish we could make it better.

She's had a better week overall. She's been on an every-other-week schedule with seizures and this past week was her week to have them. But, at the suggestion of our neurologist, we increased her morning dose of Clonapin to help control her myoclonic jerks. It seems that if we control these early enough she does not progress into full seizures. So, each morning this past week she would wake up with significant jerking and I gave her the larger dose of Clonapin. Within two hours her jerking would slow or stop and we saw no large seizures. But, she has struggled with drainage and mucus making it hard for her to breathe well. She coughs a lot and we have to suction often. We do not pull a lot out of her with suction machine and she seems to be choking on less material than normal. This may be a consequence of the Clonapin as it can make her throat muscles more relaxed and less able to deal with the amount of mucus she normally can handle. It becomes a balancing act of controlling seizures vs. letting her have stronger throat muscles.

Still, we will take the good we saw this week. She smiles in response to our interaction with her. She will even coo and wiggle in excitement. Even now, she is smiling with Jennifer as she does some chest PT to loosen up any junk in her lungs. I'm watching them on the video monitor. Macayla's smile is such a sign of her grace. She certainly has limited understanding at this point, but she maintains that smile. I would not be so composed. But it reminds me of another kind of grace, the one

Macayla gets her middle name from. God's grace. His unmerited favor and blessing. His grace is the only way our family makes it through this. His grace gives strength we do not possess. His grace not only saves us from our sins, but also teaches us to avoid sin in the future. His grace is a promise of ultimate healing and fulfillment. His grace reminds us that we are not alone. His grace moves us and others to help one another. Macayla's name is a phonetic spelling of Michaela, the feminine Hebrew for "Who is like God". It is the name given to the archangel Michael in Scripture. Macayla's life is a reflection of God's grace and she too is a messenger of His grace. Thus, her middle name is fitting. Macayla Grace is certainly a reflection of God's grace, power and love.

God's power and strength is not always demonstrated in a sudden healing. It is demonstrated in a life lived in complete dependence on his grace. My struggle to "feel good" was more than physical. It was spiritual as well. I am not a very good patient and my wife, a nurse, will testify to this fact without reservation. When I feel bad, sick or weak, I am not patient or loving. Withdrawing from an antidepressant became an opportunity for me to lean on God's grace. It was a struggle to remain patient with Jennifer and Jacob in the midst of feeling zapped and concussed. It was difficult to be "spiritual" with a seven-year-old who can be demanding while my head throbbed and my hands were numb. Patience and love do not come easily to me when I feel lousy. When I am sick, I get angry and it impacts those around me. Pain turns me into a pain for everyone else!

## WHERE THE ANSWERS ARE FOUND

It was in the midst of this I discovered God speaking an answer into my life through Scripture, sermons, prayer and reading. God began to highlight in a fresh way the need for holiness in my life. Of course, this sounds strange. Why would God want me to focus on holiness in the midst of grief? Why was God not being a little bit more sensitive to my situation? After all, I was hurting because of my daughter's death. I was struggling to wrap my mind around where we had been and where we were going. I could not even think straight because of medication withdrawals and God wanted me to focus on being holy! Really? It is at times like that we may be tempted to tell God to keep his rules to himself. We may think God is being a jerk for even bringing it up. But it is in fact one of the most loving things he can do for us.

One of the reasons we struggle with this is because we do not understand what it means to be holy. We think it involves following a list of rules and keeping up a certain appearance so that we look different from the rest of the world. We get focused on saying the right things, even if we do not understand them. We want to dress the part, look the part and speak the part, but we really do not understand the part. As John Ortberg wrote, "In other words, if we can't be *holy*, shouldn't we at least be *weird?*"[xxxvi] Holiness is often confused with adherence to a legal code. This not only keeps us from drawing closer to God, but also keeps others from drawing closer to us. We become focused on meeting superficial and sometimes banal requirements, which we create and are not biblical. Then we ignore the weightier things of our relationship with God (see Matthew 23:23). God is holy and he wants us to be holy as well. He commands it. So, how are we to understand holiness and how on earth does it help in the midst of grief or any other circumstance?

When we read through the Old Testament Law, we find God repeatedly telling his people that they should be holy for he is holy. In Deuteronomy, God repeatedly commands his people to purge the evil that is among them (see Deut. 13:5; 17:7 & 12; 19:13 & 19; 22:21-24; 24:7). The command to purge evil from Israel even involved enacting the death penalty in certain instances for those who brought evil into the Israelites' culture. Jesus said it in the strongest terms, "If your right eye makes you stumble, tear it out and throw it from you; for it is better for you to lose one of the parts of your body, than for your whole body to be thrown into hell. If your right hand makes you stumble, cut if off and throw it from you; for it is better for you to lose one of the parts of your body, than for your whole body to go into hell." (Matthew 5:29-30) This metaphor communicates how important holiness is to God and therefore important for us.

# TRIUNE HOLINESS – IT BUILDS CHARACTER

The simplest definition for holiness is "to be set apart." This means we are set apart by God for his purpose and glory. Jesus said, "If you love Me, you will keep My commandments." (John 14:15) Notice how Jesus frames obedience within a relationship of love. But this is not a new message. All of the laws in the Old Testament flow from the Ten Commandments. The Ten Commandments are the foundational outline of what holiness looks like for God's people, and they all revolve around relationships. The first four are about our relationship with God and the rest are about our relationships with others (see Exodus 20). This is why Jesus said, "'You shall love the Lord your God with all your heart, and with all your soul, and with all your mind.' This is the great and foremost commandment. The second is like it, 'You shall love your neighbor as yourself.' On these two commandments depend the whole Law and the Prophets." (Matthew 22:37-40) Holiness is lived out relationally because God is relational. Holiness is lived out through love because God is love. The Trinity describes how God is one Being and three Persons. There is an eternal relationship within God and his relational attribute is not dependent on anyone outside of himself. God the Father is always a father to the Son and God the Son is always a son to the Father. God the Spirit is always the spirit going forth from the Father and Son. There is always love between them. Creation and Scripture reveal and reflect this relational attribute of God. To be holy means we are to keep our relationships in tact and healthy. It means we share in the love that exists within the Trinity. Certainly, to continually and lovingly strengthen our relationships with God and others sets us apart!

Just after writing these words, my wife and I were speaking on the phone. She said something that stepped all over the toes of my ego. I was telling her about a contact I had made to try and drum up work. She responded with a critique of how I could have "sold" myself better. I only wanted to share with her what I had accomplished during my day. I did not need her telling me how I could have done it better. I corrected her. O.k., I snapped at her. I tried to apologize as soon as I spoke, but it was too late. The words left my mouth and there was no retrieving them. But even here, I was not truly apologizing. I really did not regret *what* I said; I only regretted how I said it. I apologized for the way I spoke but wanted to make my point to show her how wrong *she* was. I wanted her to know my anger was "righteous." But this was my ego wanting to win an argument and there is nothing righteous about it. My ego, not holiness, was governing my choices here. Holiness gives us the proper state-of-mind and state-of-heart to deal with conflict. Holiness heals relationships.

When we sin, we disrupt relationships. When we live by selfishness we put ourselves over others and we drive a wedge between them and us. When we sin against others we also sin against God. To be holy means we put our relationship with God above all else. "I am the LORD your God, who brought you out of Egypt, out of the house of slavery. You shall have no other gods before Me." (Exodus 20:2-3) When God redeems us and brings us out of slavery to sin by his work on the cross, we are in an eternal relationship with him. There are to be no other gods, no idols, no alcohol, no drugs, no entertainment, no ministry and no other relationship that takes its place. If any of these things disrupts our relationship with God, they must be radically purged from our life. If your lust causes you to stumble, cut it off and throw it away. If your anger causes you to stumble, cut it off and throw it away. If your prosperity causes you to stumble and forget God, cut it off and throw it away. If your grief causes you to stumble, cut it off and throw it away.

Our grief can either draw us closer to God or it can cause us to stumble. When we wallow in it to the point we become self-absorbed and ignore our relationship with God and others, we stumble. God showed me I needed to focus on holiness in my grief. I needed to focus on my relationship with him and others. Curling up in a ball can feel good sometimes. Certainly there are times of healthy release and cathartic bursts of emotion, but if we stay there and never come out of the fetal position, then we can fall into sin. Holiness is the answer to grief. When we get our eyes on the Author of life, death can look very different. When we learn we can actually minister to others in and through our grief, pain subsides. Holiness is not a distraction from our grief. It does not make the grief magically disappear. Holiness puts our grief in perspective and purifying our relationships with God and others gives us hope and renewed sense of the presence of Christ. This is how a true Christian can grieve with hope.

Holiness is the answer to all our circumstances, good or bad. When we put God and others first, then our perspective and contentment reach new heights. In times of prosperity, holiness makes us more thankful and generous as we know our good fortune is for God's kingdom and not our own. We can freely give and we are not trapped by selfish ambition to just get more and more. It is so easy to let our stuff control and define our lives. We buy the newest and greatest stuff and it brings a short-term high until newer and better stuff comes out.

When I was a teen, I dreamed of owning a Porsche. I had posters on my wall. I picked up magazines about these automotive marvels and thought how wonderful life would be if I had a Porsche 959. As I grew older and got married, my dream shifted to having a spectacular house. If I could just build a house the way I wanted, life would be great. But after driving normal vehicles and living in nice but modest houses by American standards, I began to realize that the more stuff I had the more problems I had. Cars breakdown. Roofs leak. Repairs are expensive. Material prosperity is not all it's cracked up to be! I also learned that as these problems surfaced, so did my character flaws. Houses, cars, electronics and such have a knack for revealing the scarcity of my patience. In the midst of dealing with these little issues, I could disrupt my relationship with my wife and children with harsh words and fits of anger. Disrupting my relationship with them disrupts my relationship with God and how shameful to realize I let this happen because of *stuff*. This is not holiness.

My father used to always say, "It builds character." That was his pat answer anytime things broke down or did not go my way. I heard this over and over and over and over again, especially in my teen years. Maybe if I buy all the stuff I want, as it breaks it will "build my character!" How's that for a spiritual growth plan? The truth is, my father is right and it reflects God's reminder to me to be holy. Holiness gives me greater perspective even for little issues in life like houses and cars. I know it is not a matter of if my car is going to break down, but when. All vehicles break down. All houses deteriorate. That silver Porsche 959 will one day rust into oblivion. That dream home will either rot down or be knocked down for someone else's project. The real question is, knowing these things happen, where will my focus remain? Holiness in prosperity means I can seek how my blessings are to be used to serve God and others. These blessings are not meant to build my kingdom but God's.

When things are not going our way, holiness also provides the perspective and contentment we need, not to mention commanded to have. When the money is gone and bills are due, is this when God wants us to turn on our spouse? When the car breaks down, is this when God wants us to yell at the kids? When we lose the job, is this when God wants us to embrace bitterness? If we live a holy lifestyle, we are living with the ever-present knowledge that everything we think, say and do is to honor and glorify God, preserving our relationship with him and others, regardless of circumstances. When we have a true relationship with God where we know him and trust him, then even the little setbacks of daily life take on new meaning. We can begin to learn and witness how God can even use those for his glory. What we think are interruptions become opportunities to serve God and grow in him. We know he will not waste those circumstances and they become opportunities to share him with others. We are transformed when we allow God and his word to inform our circumstances. In other words, it "builds character!"

While running errands in the car one afternoon, I began to think about all our family had been through. I thought of how we left a six-figure income to go to seminary. I thought of the hurricane and Macayla's situation and how I had not worked for five years to take care of her. In the middle of inventorying all my "sacrifices" for God, the Lord convicted me. He asked me to think about what he gave up for me. I thought of the throbbing pain and blood squeezing out from around the nail heads in his hands and feet. I thought of the ribbons of flesh hanging from his scourged body and the burning pain as the open air assaulted the open wounds. I thought of the gasps and screams of pain as he struggled to breathe. I thought of the utter loneliness he felt as he hung there dying on the cross for me. I discovered liberation from circumstances and stuff once I remembered that I was bought at a price. I found liberation when I realized the cost of discipleship. People think of tithing as a sacrifice but barely give ten percent. I thought I was making a real sacrifice when our income was cut in half. But Christ did not carry ten percent of the cross. He did not die for only fifty percent of my sins. He did not assume only ninety percent of humanness. He died for one hundred percent of me. He died for one hundred percent of my sins. He is not interested in a ten percent tithe. He is not interested in half of my income or five years of my life. He is interested in all of me! All of my time, all of my money, all of my thoughts, words, actions, blessings and struggles. How dare I only give him a portion when he has redeemed it all!

I was liberated from my possessions because I realized it is just stuff and it is his. My money is his money. My time is his time. Often we can feel like work, family, the house, and church are competing for our time and resources. This is why getting into Bible study can be so difficult as it feels like one more thing to add to our schedule. Going to church is one more place to be. Tithing is one more bill. But when we truly realize it all belongs to God, then there is no more competition. Work, church, family and alike all belong to God as well. When we seek his kingdom first, then making decisions about where we spend our time and resources becomes straightforward. Spending time in God's word becomes as normal as eating because without it we starve. The more time we spend in God's word and prayer, the clearer decisions become regardless of their size. We find patience to wait on God's timing in decisions. We find perspective on what is important and this helps to prioritize. Amazingly, what we thought was so important before can often become simple and much less stressful. We also discover where we have neglected the weightier things of life. Seeking and preserving our relationship with God and others first is holiness and it gives us what we need in all circumstances.

Just to be clear and honest, I am not super-spiritual or perfect at maintaining this perspective. I obviously needed this reminder driving in the car that day, tallying my sacrifices, and I need it everyday. This is why we must deny ourselves and take up our cross *daily*. We must go to the cross of Christ everyday and not in some routine, ritualistic way. Each day, even each hour, we must size up our circumstances in light of the cross. These blood-soaked beams of wood can put our pain, frustrations and challenges in the proper perspective. The empty, hewed-out rock of the tomb puts our successes, blessings and future in the proper perspective as well. This proper perspective is not that these circumstances are unimportant or can simply be glossed over. Instead, these circumstances become clearly assessed and prioritized. The coworker who grates on every nerve and fiber of our being can finally be seen as a human being, made in the image of God, needing a Savior like us. The sudden unemployment we face becomes an opportunity to see God provide in ways we never imagined. The death of a loved one can become a chance to see that death has ultimately lost its sting and full power, for our Savior has overwhelmed the grave (1 Cor. 15:50-58).

This may sound nice in theory, but when we lose a loved one, it does sting. It can shake our hearts to the core and crush us. God says he has taken death's sting and victory away and promises to fully crush it in the end (1 Cor. 15:25-26). In the meantime, we are called to be holy and put up with death's shadow and the pain it causes. How does this help? In our situation, the grief came because our daughter died. Death obviously disrupts a relationship in a severe way, thus it hurts so much. Focusing on holiness means focusing on relationships, but how was I supposed to do that with Macayla gone? How can I be sure that death has lost its victory and will one day be completely abolished?

Previously, I described a time early on in the disease when Macayla was having multiple seizures and how understandable it is that people could confuse epilepsy and demon possession. In the midst of those seizures, I sobbed with my face buried in the comforter of Macayla's bed. Out of the blue, I felt Macayla's hand gently patting my head trying to comfort me. Her seizures had stopped and she was clear and not glazed over in convulsions. After the funeral, once the anti-depressant was almost out of my system, I lay in Macayla's bed and sobbed. I cried for almost an hour, eyes slammed shut in pain and tears. Out of the blue, it felt as if Macayla was in the room with me, standing next to the bed, patting me on the head once again. She was standing! She was aware! She was beautiful! I opened my eyes but she was not physically there. I am not claiming her ghost came for a visit. But I believe God used a memory and tweaked it to give me a sense of comfort. I believe God tailored an experience using something from my past to let me know Mac was o.k. She was no longer hurting. She was whole and with a newfound, eternal perspective, she even knew my pain was but a moment. God let me see in my mind's eye that Macayla was where all hope and faith are realized in full. She could not come back to me, but I would go to her one day. The reality was that death had not disrupted our relationship. We may have been separated by a veil between the portion of reality where I am and the rest of reality where Macayla is, but our relationship was intact and even stronger. This strengthened my hope.

In this hope, I am discovering how David could rise, clean himself up and go to worship after his son died. I am discovering afresh the mediator Job so longed for who is Christ Jesus. I am discovering how Macayla was born, Battens and all, for the glory of God and that I am not angry with him for it. I am discovering the Father who lost his Son and the Son who suffered more than I can know. Because of his great love for us, the Son was forsaken at the cross to pay the infinite debt we owe for our sin. This love is not simply an emotion, but a knowledge and action. This is not love written on a greeting card, but written in blood on the hearts and minds of God's people. His subsequent victory over death at the tomb is shared with Macayla and all who belong to him. I am discovering again Macayla and our family are gently held in his strong, nail-scarred hands because we belong to him. To allow grief to disrupt such a relationship would indeed be blasphemous and destructive. Holiness is helping me find the answers to "why" for both my heart and mind.

The Lord struck the child. How we recoil at the very thought! But our perspective is short on holiness. For David's child, he left this life and went quickly into the presence of God. His life, short though it was, had a greater purpose and was part of redemptive history. This child had more impact in seven days for God's people than most do in a lifetime. We wish it were different. God intended it to be different, thus he cried at the tomb of his friend, Lazarus. But when love is a choice as it was in the Garden of Eden, so is selfishness. Through selfishness sin and death entered the world. Let us never forget the Lord did nothing to this child he did not do to his own. Let us not forget the selfless act of Jesus. Let us not forget the wrath poured out at the cross. Jesus, humanly speaking was also a son of David. He was struck infinitely more on Calvary than David's other son, the child of Bathsheba. Thanks be to God for the sons of David! Both were innocents. Both were struck. The little one helped set the stage for the great One. He changed everything so we can be made new and holy. Powering this holiness is his amazing love for us.

## SELF-ASSESSMENT

1. Do you consider your circumstances as an opportunity to see what Christ is doing and share that with others? If not, why?
2. How do you let disappointment impact your relationship with those closest to you?
3. What do you think is your biggest barrier to consistent Bible study? If not having enough time is the barrier; does your time belong to God?
4. Think of all you have in money, time, stuff, family and friends. What percentage of these do you honestly consider as belonging to God?
5. In what way can you apply holiness (seeking and preserving your relationship with God and others) to your current situation?

# 9

# Signs

## *The Story of a Community*

I sat in the lobby of a Montgomery, Alabama hotel and watched the morning weather report. Tropical storm Bonnie was on track to hit New Orleans. Five years earlier, our family evacuated to this same hotel to escape hurricane Katrina. This time we were on our way back to New Orleans to visit the New Orleans Baptist Theological Seminary campus. The trip was part of the process to seek God's direction for our family. Were we to move back to New Orleans now that Macayla had gone Home? Were we to pick up where we left off before Battens disease? Tropical storm Bonnie was going to hit New Orleans two days after we were to arrive. Katrina hit two weeks after we moved in the first time. Was Bonnie a sign from God to stay away?

In 2005, we heard from several people hurricane Katrina was a sign from God that we should not have been in New Orleans and Macayla's diagnosis was sign to never go back. A few people did not even appeal to God. They simply believed it was foolish to move to a city that was below sea level on the Gulf Coast. For them, hurricane Katrina was simply proof of their wisdom. Watching the projected path of Bonnie brought all of these comments back to the surface. Granted it was simply a tropical storm and not a hurricane yet, but it was eerily taking a path similar to Katrina. How were we to respond?

We continued on our trip to New Orleans and Bonnie all but evaporated when she came on shore. In fact, it made that Sunday morning quite comfortable with a little extra cloud cover. So, was this a sign? Was God telling us he would protect us from hurricanes if we came to New Orleans again? On the other hand, was God letting us off easy with a mild warning of what was going to happen again? Obviously, determining God's will via circumstances is misguided. Depending on our emotional state, indigestion, or whims we can interpret our circumstances in all sorts of ways and this is extremely foolish. Watching that weather report in the hotel lobby stirred a strange feeling in me. Was that feeling a sign from God or was that just the garlic-mashed potatoes I had the night before? The real focus should not be on the "sign" value of circumstances. Instead we need to focus on our expectations, especially our expectations of relationships. We need to focus on how our response to circumstances impacts our relationship with others and God. We must temper that focus with God's Word.

## PRIDE, THE RELATIONSHIP KILLER

I went into law enforcement right out of college. I loved the work and the opportunities to help people. It is a unique profession. On a daily basis, law enforcement officers meet total strangers who are in the midst of major failures and struggles. While considering all of the human issues and relationships involved in these circumstances, the officers must also weigh out the legal and constitutional issues. Then there are the direct dangers of weapon-wielding suspects, high-speed vehicle maneuvers and dynamic conflicts. Split-second decisions must be made and these decisions carry ramifications involving liability, constitutional liberties, life and death. There is also the mountain of documentation that must accompany these decisions. Crime dramas on television accomplish in one hour what takes years in the criminal justice system. Needless to say, law enforcement is a stressful line of work and this stress impacts not only the officers, but also their families.

I was in law enforcement when Jennifer and I met and we struggled through this during our first year of marriage. Part of my struggle stemmed from the fact I was attempting to rationalize away God's call on my life to go into ministry. In the meantime, I watched the marriages of other officers around me disintegrate. I saw officers having affairs and leaving their spouses. The divorce rate in law enforcement has been estimated to be between sixty to seventy-five percent compared to the national average of around fifty percent.[xxvii]

In short, I saw the cards were stacked against us for a successful marriage so I made a career change and went into construction. It seemed like a natural fit as I grew up on construction sites. My father has been a contractor for as long as I can remember. As a child, I would go with him to the local diner before school so he could find out the scoop on jobs and potential work. I was the only child sitting among these flannel-clad coffee guzzlers as they told sordid jokes and gossiped about local work and those doing it. The smell of bacon mingled with my coffee, which was loaded with sugar and cream to make it palatable to my young taste buds. These men seemed like giants sitting around a table. Throughout my childhood and teen years, I learned not only how to drive the nails and build, but how to draw blueprints and estimate. As an adult, construction was a comfortable place so I went back into it with hopes of making more money and starting a stable family. I began meeting this goal, however I could not outrun God's call on my life.

My relationship with him kept this calling before me and it was stressful. I knew I was not doing what I was supposed to be. I tried to bargain with God and remind him how often I was able to share the Gospel on construction sites. I shared the Gospel with men like the ones I sat with as a child in the diner, and they *really* needed a Savior, right? But God was not open to my negotiations or my prideful assessment of others. So, I started seminary. Ironically, I ended up as a stay-at-home father of a special-needs child. I was told the divorce rate for special-needs families was even higher than law enforcement families. We jumped out of the frying pan and landed in the fire! It seems statisticians cannot find agreement on the actual numbers, but it is certainly understandable if the divorce rate is higher due to the stresses special-needs care can bring to a marriage. But the issue is deeper than stats and numbers.

It is easy to allow statistics to influence us. One of the main reasons I left law enforcement was to protect our marriage from the divorce rate. When we heard special-needs families are subject to an eighty-percent divorce rate, it was easy to feel our marriage was doomed. Even the fifty percent statistic for all marriage is overwhelming if we pause long enough to ponder it. However, statistics do not cause divorce. Stresses of law enforcement, special needs or even finances do not cause divorce. Divorce, like all broken relationships, is rooted in pride. This is not the pride associated with the admiration and appreciation a parent has for their child. This pride is the same pride found in the Garden of Eden at the Tree of Knowledge. This pride is an ultimate selfishness in which we make ourselves the center of the universe and kick all others, including God, to the curb. This is the pride from which all other sin flows. Law enforcement officers run into this pride on almost every call and find they are not immune to it either. I struggle with this pride on a daily basis as does my wife and children. Pride leads us to attempt planning out every detail of our lives as if we are sovereign. I was going to save our marriage and make lots of money by going into construction and ignore God's call on my life! It is in pride relationships are damaged and sometimes destroyed.

There are times when we feel as if no one can understand our situation or circumstances. We can even hear of others in circumstances similar to our own and say, "Yes, but my situation is different because..." Certainly, there are unique details to every person's situation, but others have experienced our overall circumstance. In our pride, we can make more of our suffering than we ought because of a lack of perspective.

At times, I found myself withdrawing from other families affected by Battens disease. Sometimes I did not want to hear about their challenges and deep down I could sense my resistance toward them. It was a subtle and almost imperceptible emotional response and closely related to envy. In those moments, I would listen to their woes and try to encourage, but in some deep recess of my heart I was discounting their struggles as less difficult than mine. Simultaneously, I could think prideful thoughts that these other parents did not have a handle on the situation like me. Fortunately, this was a rare feeling and by the grace of God I was able to be sincerely concerned about others most of the time. Pride is a devious and surreptitious force in our spirit and it destroys when it is not resisted.

Pride is focused completely on self while holiness is focused on God and others. Holiness is defined as being set apart by God and the Ten Commandments are a portrait of what this setting apart looks like. These commandments are centered on our relationship with God and others. If this is true, we need to explore how this plays out in daily life. It may be helpful to consider what unholiness looks like and when it typically rears its head. To do this, we will explore the story of a community. This community lived two thousand years ago and in it were some of the first Christians. The apostle Peter wrote a letter to them we call First Peter. It addresses the struggles of this ancient group of people with their familial and cultural relationships. This letter encouraged them in the midst of hostile and uncertain circumstances. The Holy Spirit, through Peter, gave these early Christians and all those who came after what we need in any situation. Let us focus on God's word, not statistics or circumstances, for direction.

## HOLINESS, THE PRIDE KILLER

There are many Christians in America concerned about increased hostility toward Christianity in our culture, but we have yet to face hostility on the level of Peter's audience. His epistle is addressed to Christians scattered throughout what is known today as Turkey. These believers faced a culture we can scarcely imagine in our comfortable churches and freedom. Jews who converted to Christianity faced both social and economic hardship as they were often excommunicated from the synagogue and surrounding community. This affected social, familial and economic standing. As Christians spread across the Roman Empire, they faced a hostile pagan culture as well. The early Christians were often called atheists because they did not believe in the gods of the Greco-Roman culture. They did not participate in the public festivals to these gods but worshiped privately. Christians were often not accepted into the culture:

> They were popularly charged with perpetrating the grossest immoralities in their conventicles. It was said that both sexes met together at night, that a dog was used to extinguish the lights, and that promiscuous intercourse followed. Garbled reports circulated of the central Christian rite, the Eucharist. The fact that it was celebrated only in the presence of believers fed the rumours that Christians regularly sacrificed an infant and consumed its blood and flesh. The circumstance

that Christians called one another brother and sister and loved one another on the scantiest acquaintance was regarded as evidence of vice.[xxviii]

Though not everyone saw Christians with such disdain, their failure to participate in the cultural events had economic impact that could be noticed on the local level. They typically did not purchase the meat sacrificed to pagan gods and they did not worship the Emperor. This lack of participation brought suspicion and distrust. It could even stir fears among the pagans that the gods would punish their community for allowing these "atheists" to remain. Some in our culture accuse Christians of being strange, but comparatively Christians in the first and second century were considered a cult of dissenters and haters of the human race.

The net result of this cultural collision was persecution and ostracism for the first Christians. Persecutions in the first and second centuries were not typically official government policy, with the possible exception of Nero and a few others, but most often occurred among the people. From the New Testament itself we have the record of Stephen's execution (Acts 7), Peter's near execution (Acts 12), Paul's persecutions and near death experiences (Acts 13, 14, 16, 22), and references throughout the epistles of the difficulties Christians faced. The struggles ranged from lethal to social sneers. There was a cost to wearing the label of Christian in that time and culture. In our present culture, the cost of this label is so minimal that many flippantly apply it to themselves. Most wear this label today as nothing more than a cultural designation. They went to a Christian church on occasion as a child. They celebrate Christmas (albeit more about Santa Clause, Christmas trees and family reunion than about Christ). They simply state a belief in God and assume that makes them a Christian. However, James even pointedly wrote, "You believe that God is one. You do well; the demons also believe, and shudder." (2:19) The earliest Christians had to draw a line in the sand and so do we. Holiness is found on Christ's side of that line while pride is found on the culture's side.

The central message of 1 Peter is that we remain holy in all circumstances. The letter starts off by recapping the redemptive work of the Trinity and the permanence and immeasurable value of this redemption (1:1-12). From there Peter quickly goes to the thesis of the letter:

> Therefore, prepare your minds for action, keep sober in spirit, fix your hope completely on the grace to be brought to you at the revelation of Jesus Christ. As obedient children, do not be conformed to the former lusts which were yours in your ignorance, but like the Holy One who called you, be holy yourselves also in all your behavior; because it is written, "You shall be holy for I am holy." (1 Peter 1:13-16)

Peter tells us to "prepare [our] minds for action" or literally in the Greek to "gird up the loins of our mind." This was a figure of speech akin to our idea of "rolling up our sleeves." Christians are not to throw their brains in the trash but exactly the opposite. Thus, we are to be "sober in spirit" or clear thinking and self-controlled, something Peter repeats twice more in this letter. We are not called to prepare our minds for vacation, naïve faith, or to feel our way through things. We are to think, and think clearly. Most importantly, we are to be holy and not seek to satisfy the whimsical lusts of our culture. Through pride, our culture can take wonderful gifts from God such as food, sex, and rest and twist them into vices and destructive forces. Notice how Peter states that conformity to these lusts occurs in ignorance, not in clear and informed thinking.

## HOPE IN HOLINESS

In the midst of stress, it is easy to cope by repeated trips to the pantry. I found myself there over and over during Macayla's life and death. It was easier to walk to the fridge, pantry or call for Chinese take-out than to get on my knees in prayer. It was easier to satisfy my stomach for a quick sensation of comfort than to go before the throne of God. Going before God seemed to be hard work compared to a quick snack. It also meant I would have to face some of my weaknesses or flaws. That is uncomfortable anytime and how much more when I am seeking comfort. But on a deeper level, I simply did not trust God to actually comfort me. I knew intellectually from what I read in Scripture that God comforts, but I did not trust him to do so. Part of our problem stems from the cultural tendency toward instant gratification. If we pray to God for comfort and do not experience an instant washing of the warm-and-fuzzies, then chocolate ice cream or sesame chicken quickly become our preferred remedy. My coping mechanisms have changed over time and unfortunately God has rarely been one of them. Our culture offers so many tantalizing options for pleasure and these become our comforters. Sexual gratification, consumerism, sports, media, games, drugs, alcohol; the list is virtually endless. But Peter, speaking to those struggling to remain faithful in much harsher conditions than ours, tells us the offerings of our culture will not bring true comfort or hope.

He tells us to not fix our hope on circumstances, sesame chicken or even the promise of future, material prosperity, for these are transient. We are to *completely* hope in the grace of Christ and through Christ this grace is being revealed more and more. Our hope and comfort comes from Jesus and not from our culture, food, sexual gratification or material prosperity. These pleasures are not evidence of God's grace, hope or holiness. Pain is not evidence of a lack of God's grace, hope or holiness either. Our hope is fueled by revelation, the revelation of God's grace, not circumstances. If we place our hope in the great job we have, where does that hope go when we are transferred or laid off? If we place our hope in our spouse, where does it go when our spouse fails us? Christ never fails. Christ is not undone by bad moods, bad economies, hurricanes or even deadly diseases.

God's grace and hope are evidenced by what Christ has done, is doing and will do. Knowing and experiencing this truth is crucial and Peter gives us how this happens. He refers to his audience as "obedient children." He presupposes their identity as children of God and will even challenge them to remember this in verse 17. It is the relationship that is the crucial starting point. Are you a child of God? If so, "nothing can separate us from the love of Christ, neither death nor life, nor angels, nor principalities, nor things present, nor things to come, nor powers, nor height, nor depth, nor any other created thing will be able to separate us from the love of God, which is Jesus Christ our Lord." (Rom. 8:38-39) This is the grace on which we fix our hope. This is the relationship from which our holiness comes.

Peter tells us that all of our behavior is to be holy. All. Every action in every situation is to be holy. He even quotes the phrase so common in the Old Testament Law, "You shall be holy for I am holy." Notice it did not say, "You shall be holy except for when you are really grieved, hurt, upset or depressed, for I am holy." Nor did it say, "You shall be holy except when you are really enjoying yourself on the golf course, for I am holy." In every situation, every action is to be holy. If every action in every situation is going to be holy, then those actions must flow out of more than a legal code or religious zeal; mere outward appearances are not good enough for God. Thus, Peter brings up the nature of our relationship with God in verse 17. "If you address as Father the One who impartially judges according to each one's work, conduct yourselves in fear during the time of your stay on earth…" Notice the fact that we can have the intimacy of a Father-child relationship with the Judge of the universe. God is the ultimate standard of holiness and purity and only through an actual relationship with him can we share in this holiness.

Peter gives us various examples of how this holiness looks in all our behavior. We can be thankful Scripture gives us direct examples like these as our time here is short, or as Peter quotes, "All flesh is like grass, and all its glory like the flower of grass. The grass withers, and the flower falls off, but the word of the LORD endures forever." (1 Peter 1:24-25) Scripture helps us get it right. Peter begins with general terms of behavior and attitude. We are to put aside ALL malice, deceit, hypocrisy, envy and slander but, like newborns long for milk, we are to long for God's word. It is what we need to grow into the salvation that has been given to us (2:1-3). If we are truly God's children, then we are part of something much bigger than our circumstances. God is building his kingdom with us and in a metaphor of construction, which I can appreciate, we are living stones being assembled together to build a spiritual house. Christ himself is the foundational cornerstone of this project and all the other stones must line up along his bearings (2:4-10). Thus, our behavior is to be excellent, even among those who hate us as well as those we do not like (2:11-25). It is tempting to read these exhortations and agree with them intellectually or theologically while considering them too lofty to be incorporated into daily life.

Therefore, we often slice and dice the Bible into different compartments and levels according to our comfort and preferences. The parts of the Bible that seem "reasonable" and bring comfort or encouragement are the parts we more readily take to heart. We like that Christ came to bring the abundant life (John 10:10) but we may ignore the call he gave us to take up our own cross and follow him daily. We may think the Great Commission in Matthew 28:19-20 was just for the first disciples or missionaries and miss that all believers in all places and times were given this command. We will quote the second greatest commandment, "Love your neighbor as you love yourself," but forget the first and greatest commandment, "You shall love the Lord your God with all your heart, mind, soul and strength," (Mark 12:28-34)

In fact, we may even go from slicing and dicing to outright surgical precision in what parts and verses we pull out. Often people say, "God will not give you more than you are able to bear." The idea being that God will not allow circumstances to come into your life you cannot handle. This sounds good and syncs well with our comfort-addicted, self-help culture. Those who make this statement are surgically proof-texting and paraphrasing from 1 Corinthians 10:13 which actually states:

> No *temptation* has overtaken you but such as is common to man; and God is faithful, who will not allow you *to be tempted* beyond what you are able, *but with the temptation will provide the way of escape also, so that you will be able to endure it.* (emphasis added)

This verse is speaking of temptations, not circumstances. The issue of temptation is central to the chapter's context. More importantly, God allows in the temptations in a believer's life, but at the same time he provides the grace to resist them. The point of this section of Scripture is to flee from sin and rely on the sufficient sacrifice of Christ on the cross to forgive our sins. We are to rely on the grace he freely gives us to live a holy life. In no way is there a promise that God keeps our hardships to a minimum. It was more than I could bear to lose Macayla and not only lose her, but watch her suffer through so much first. It was more than Job could bear to lose everything and have to sit through thirty-three chapters worth of arguing over his righteousness. God often gives us more than we can handle so that we may grow to rely on him more. The fact is, apart from God, these circumstances would have consumed us and become the very thing that defines our lives. At the core of the Gospel message is the fact that humans cannot withstand temptation or trials, not even believers, without the grace God provides.

## HOLY BOUNCE BACK

When we experience life-changing suffering, we can often "bounce back" from such times by investing our lives to help others in similar circumstances. This is one of the great things that can result from tragedy, though we must not assume this is the *reason* for our tragedy. We are to comfort others with the comfort we ourselves have received (2 Cor. 1:3-5). But even here, we must make sure that our circumstances are not defining our lives more than Christ. If you have lost a child, it can become a mission of sorts to help families with dying children. Recovering alcoholics can help other alcoholics find recovery. Some of the parents we know with special-needs children have started organizations and fundraisers to help others with similar conditions. As wonderful as these efforts are, we can let them become all-consuming and prevent us from growing in Christ if they are not handled correctly and biblically. Even a desire to bring about good things can sometimes lead to idolatry. Our special-needs organization can become more focused on our mission and ability and less focused on honoring Christ. It can become more about our glory than God's. Recovering addicts may discover how helpful Scripture is and begin to memorize it. But the process of memorizing and regurgitating Scripture can become an addiction in itself and the verses memorized are not studied or understood. They become nothing more than a string of words. But when in group with other addicts or while at church, we can enjoy the recognition we receive for our memorization skills and righteous appearance. It can become more about our glory than God's. It is easy for our good works to become the main source of our comfort instead of seeking our comfort in the Comforter. We can actually take a great thing and twist it into an idol.

I am not in anyway suggesting we stop doing good works, but pragmatic good is not the only thing God desires for us. Peter writes of the good things we are to do in his letter from 2:1 to 3:12, but he brings us back to the source in 3:15, "but sanctify Christ as Lord in your hearts, always being ready to make a defense to everyone who asks you to give an account for the hope that is in you, yet with gentleness and reverence." If Christ is sanctified, or set apart, in our hearts, then he is the Lord of our life and we are not. We cannot sit on the throne he already occupies. When we live out these good things in front of people, Peter points out that they will notice. But are they noticing Christ or us? If they ask us to explain why we do what we do, will we explain that Christ is the source of our hope and subsequent impact, or will we only speak of ourselves? It is easier to point to the pragmatic benefits of any good we may do. "We raised $10,000 for cancer research," or "I've helped twenty other guys find recovery from their addiction." Peter wrote we each have received a specific gift or ability and we should employ it in serving others but "whoever speaks is to do so as one who is speaking the utterances of God; whoever serves is to do so as one who is serving by the strength which God supplies; so that in all things God may be glorified through Jesus Christ, to whom belongs the glory and dominion forever and ever. Amen." (see 1 Peter 4:10-11).

## REALISTIC HOLINESS

We must notice that Peter's list of good works in this letter are all relationship based. It is about how we relate to our government, our employers or masters, our spouse and with those who hate us. He will even expand this in chapter five to relationships within the Church. Those relationships must be shaped by one ultimate relationship, our relationship with Christ. If he is not the Lord of our hearts and minds, then all we accomplish will ultimately be for another lord, namely ourselves. Our good works are meant to create and strengthen relationships with others and hopefully lead them to a relationship with Christ. So, our good works are meant to equally accomplish two things: first, that through them we love the Lord our God with all our heart, mind, soul and strength and grow closer to him; second, that we love our neighbors as ourselves, meeting their needs and ultimately showing them the relationship they can have with Christ. Then they repeat the process through their lives.

Being holy in all things is not an unrealistic demand from God because of the grace we have in Christ. It is not always easy, but it is a realistic demand and it has far reaching implications. It can only start with a proper relationship with Christ. He must be the Lord of our lives, not simply a Savior. We like that he would save us, but we are not so sure we want him to be our boss. But we really cannot separate these two functions of Christ, for if he is our Savior then he is our Lord. For we "were not redeemed with perishable things like silver and gold from our futile way of life…but with the precious blood, as of a lamb, unblemished and spotless, the blood of Christ." (see 1 Peter 1:18-19) In other words, if he is our Savior, we are bought and paid for. We are no longer our own but our lives, time, efforts, blessings and abilities all belong to him.

This can be extremely difficult to keep in perspective when our good works are so personally relevant to our own lives. I have to constantly pray that this book stay focused on Christ first and not put me, Macayla, our family or anything else in front of him. Because of our desire to help others who hurt like we do, we can take our eyes off of the Author and Perfecter of our faith. Then, by default, our faith will be in someone or something else. When we are truly children of God, then holiness becomes a possibility for our lives that apart from Christ could not exist. The demand to be holy does not remain unreasonable or so lofty that we can just wave it off. It is not a piece of "pie-in-the-sky" Scripture that is optional but is, in fact, foundational to all we will ever think, say or do as a child of God.

Circumstances change and certainly God is involved in them, orchestrating, sustaining and ordaining events. However, God also gave us Scripture through which we can interpret and understand our circumstances. Scripture reveals God and His purposes. The first question we must ask anytime we read Scripture is, "What does this teach me about God and his character?" The clearer we see God, then the clearer we see ourselves, both as we are and as he intends us to be. Once we have that in view it puts our circumstances and our lives in the proper perspective. Tropical storm Bonnie was simply a sign of rough weather and that it was hurricane season. But God's word and much prayer was telling us to return to New Orleans. Even if another storm hit, it would simply be a storm. It would be tragic and mean we may be in the right place to minister to some hurting people. There were still people hurting from Katrina even five years after the fact and we were looking forward to ministering to them as well. Storms come and go, but God's word is constant. God's word helps us to better understand, cope and respond to all our circumstances.

However, is it foolish to move to a city that could flood with the slightest nudge from a hurricane? Certainly, it is not what we would prefer. If we were simply looking for a place to live, then a place like New Orleans would not be high on our list. We would prefer to be serving God in a posh, comfortable and safe place. Why go where the murder rate per capita is ten times the national average? Why live where a storm could take everything away? It only makes sense to go because God said to go. We know he said go because we searched his word and prayed through it. We went through the process of prayer, Bible study and worship to come to this conclusion five years earlier and we repeated the process for our trip back. We did not come to this conclusion because of circumstances. We did not simply feel our way through it, but had to prepare our minds for action and be sober in spirit. We did not make this decision by throwing our brains in the trash but by remembering to love the Lord our God with all our heart, mind, soul and strength. This is difficult at times. We can feel close to God at times, but not think clearly about Scripture's description of him. At other moments, we can think clearly about precepts in the Bible and intellectually grasp its truth without letting it impact our heart. We can forget that our whole person and all our effort are to be used to strengthen our relationship with him. Recognizing these potential pitfalls, we were better able to wade through the prayer, worship and Scripture and discover God's next step for us was to go back to New Orleans.

Scripture reveals God rarely calls people to a comfortable and posh purpose. God sometimes calls prophets to seemingly nicer assignments. Isaiah and Nathan were called to minister directly kings in palaces. But they were called to minister to some very difficult situations and deliver some bad news quite often. Certainly we would prefer palaces to the evil cities like Nineveh or New Orleans. But when God became flesh in Jesus Christ, he came to a hard life, rejected and misunderstood by many. After three years of ministry and miracles, he had 120 disciples in Jerusalem. Definitely not a mega-church! He went to a literal Hell on earth at the cross where the just wrath our sins deserve was placed on him and not us. This was certainly not "Your Best Life Now" kind of Christianity! There was no smiling at the cross! Christ died at the cross, but rose from the tomb. He called us to take up our crosses and follow him. If that means we have to go to places that are not comfortable or even dangerous, then that is where we go. This does not mean we throw our brain in the trashcan. That is not faith. It means we are to utilize our brains and see what God tells us in his word and act on it. Peter's first-century audience needed this clarity as they faced God's uncomfortable, cross-bearing purpose for their lives. Our need is no different.

Tropical storm Bonnie was not a sign. The sign we have is called Scripture. Like all signs, it points to something, or in this case, someone, beyond itself. We do not worship Scripture, but the One to whom it points. It is through this relationship we see our situations, sin, and lives with clarity. It helps us wade through storms, be it hurricane or Battens disease. When rightly divided and earnestly sought, God's word gives us answers, even the portions that can be most troubling to us. "The Lord struck the child" is certainly troubling, but no more than the cry from the cross, "My God, My God, why have You forsaken Me?" We can look to these perplexing texts and find clarity when we allow God to speak to us through them and stop relying on our circumstances to guide us. Let our minds and hearts be illuminated!

## SELF-ASSESSMENT

1. What portions of the Bible have you chosen to ignore?
2. How do you expect God to speak to you?
3. What choices are you facing right now? Are you responding or reacting? Is your response or reaction based on your desires or God's? How can you know?
4. Do you trust God knowing that he will allow circumstances into your life beyond your own ability or strength to bear?
5. Are you responding more to culture or Scripture? In other words, are you allowing the culture or Scripture to shape you into the person you are?

# 10
# Becoming Like a Child
## *The Story of Jacob*

During our journey with Macayla, my wife's aunt, Debbie Sherman, helped us by maintaining our website. As mentioned before, it started as a way to keep family and friends up to date, but expanded into a ministry outlet. Smoaksignal.com included a prayer request page, photos, contact points, information on Battens, blogs, and a page dedicated to our son, Jacob. Each month I tried to add stories to his page. Some were funny and cute. Some were profound and showed us how God used Jacob through this journey. Jacob can help us see how to live as a disciple of Christ. He can helps us see how holiness is the answer to our struggles.

In February 2008, I posted following on Jacob's page:

> The last couple of months have been hectic and I think Jacob has had to spend too much time with his Dad. My attitude got a check the other day when we were riding together in the van. We were pressed for time so I apparently was not being very personable.
> 
> Jacob said, "It must be pretty boring to be a father."
> 
> I asked what he meant.
> 
> He responded, "It must be boring to be a father because you have to take care of kids all the time."
> 
> I assured him that being a father was not boring, maybe difficult at times, but not boring. I took some time to think about what led him to this

conclusion. My attitude was obviously teaching him *something* about fathers.

To top it off, the next day he comes to me out of the blue and says, "Dad, I CAN wait to be a grown up. Being a grown up is not much fun so I can wait."

His perception and wisdom was convicting. Being a grown up does not mean we should lose the wonder of life, but I obviously reflected that loss of wonder to Jacob. It is also convicting that as a father I was being a poor reflection of the heavenly Father that I want to point Jacob to. I pray that I can regain that wonder and let it be contagious for Jacob.

Ravi Zacharias wrote, "How, then, does one retain a sense of wonder without being permanently entranced?...How does one take the emotional high points and successfully balance them with the sharp edges of sorrow that are also part of life?"[xxix] Zacharias goes on to point out the answer lies in a miracle only Christ can perform. It is a miracle that occurs when we allow ourselves to be filled with Christ and his instruction. As a husband and father of two, I believe one of my roles is to help my family discover this truth. Jacob has served as a check and challenge of my role. If my son never wants to grow up because he sees adulthood as drudgery, then I have not done my job. Worst of all, I have not loved my son if I have not done all I can to point him toward Christ and Christ's purpose for his life. Just as I teach him that playing in the street is dangerous and food is a great blessing, I must teach him there are bigger, eternal dangers and blessings to face.

## GROW UP!

There is a story of twins recorded in Genesis 25. Esau was born first with his twin, Jacob, holding on to his heel. Jacob's name means "one who takes by the heel or supplants." (It was a good thing Jacob was not picking his nose when he came out. I don't know what the Hebrew is for "nose picker" but it would have been a harsh name to live with! That is a child who would beg to be home schooled!) Esau was still the firstborn and as such had rights above and ahead of Jacob. However, Jacob lived up to his name as an adult and supplanted his older brother through trickery. He traded Esau a bowl of stew for the birthright! Both brothers failed miserably here. Esau traded who he was for a temporary, physical comfort and Jacob tried to become something he was not in order to get ahead. He tried to sidestep the role in which he had been placed. Later, Jacob had to face God and come to grips with his deceptions. Here is where God changed his name to Israel, or "one who strives with God." Jacob fought who he was and his place in life. He made sinful choices in trying to circumvent the path and relationships God had for him. But God did not write him off. God brought Jacob to a new place and a new identity.

In some respects, our Jacob has had to grow up fast. He spent his first seven years of life watching his big sister deteriorate and die. Our Jacob is also a "trickster" as some translate the name. I will not admit where he gets this trait! But Jacob is also a supplanter, though not through treachery. Jacob had to slowly become the big brother as Macayla digressed. He had to watch out for her and often give up what he wanted for her needs. It may seem tragic he had to go through this, but God did not waste it. God has and will always use it in Jacob's life. He strives with God in his own way and has asked why Macayla had to be on this path. Jacob's questions and struggles have challenged us as parents and made us earnestly assess what we believe. When you are forced to explain complex and deep issues to a child, it challenges you to learn and learn deeply.

Often, parents struggle with their children's questions about God, suffering, sin, and the Bible. We often try to dumb it down for the kids, that is, if we are bold enough to even try to answer their questions. Since these subjects are complex for us, we rationalize they are too complicated and abstract for children to grasp. We do not understand the Trinity, so how could a child? We do not understand why there is suffering, so how could a child? We do not draw clear lines of morality in our own lives, so how can we for our children? These subjects are heavy and at times complex, but that does not mean we cannot have a biblical understanding of them. God does not require us to become expert theologians and philosophers, but he does require us to learn what is in his word.

Most Americans who label themselves as Christians own several Bibles but cannot tell you where their Bibles are much less what is written inside. Those who, for the first time, begin to seek God in his word and prayer may possibly discover they have only been a nominal or cultural Christian but not an actual Christ-follower. The average, church-going Christian who takes the time to actually read the Bible is in the minority. If the average church-going Christian not only reads but also studies the Bible, they are in an even smaller minority. But they are the ones who are better equipped to teach their children. They are better equipped to face the challenges of life. Notice it does not mean we escape those challenges. Studying Scripture and prayer does not exempt us from trials, but it draws us closer to our Creator and this provides something more substantial than simple pain relief. Unfortunately, we get into the habit of opening our Bible to find a quick answer to the problem currently on our plate. We call that "Bible study." If we don't find the answer instantly, we assume Bible study doesn't "work." Studying the Bible means we camp out on a section of text and do some digging to find out why it was written. It means we search for not only the meaning of individual words in their original context, but also how that translates and applies to our situation. Most importantly, it means we dig deeper to discover what a text is teaching us about God. How can we offer to our children what we do not possess ourselves? It is not the children who do not understand; it is the adults.

## THE SET-UP FOR MATURITY

Jesus' disciples once asked him, "Who is the greatest person in the kingdom of heaven?" (Matthew 18:1). In ironic immaturity, they wanted to know which one of them was the most honorable and mature. Their question was raised out of what they had just witnessed (see Matthew 17). Jesus gave a glimpse of his glory to Peter, James and John during his transfiguration on a mountaintop. They saw Jesus standing there in glorious light with Moses and Elijah. It was an amazing sight. Jesus then came down from the mountain and cast out a demon his other disciples were unable to budge due to a lack of faith and understanding. By this point, the disciples were somewhat humbled and truly amazed. They must have wanted some of this power for themselves. However, Jesus told them as they continued in their travels that he would be delivered into the hands of men and killed. He told them he would rise on the third day. They went from amazing miracles to talk of death.

When they reached Capernaum, a tax collector asked Peter if Jesus paid the annual temple tax. See the irony! He was asking God the Son if he paid the tax for the very place he was to be worshiped! But Peter, not thinking in these terms, answered for Jesus and said, "Yes." If anything, after hearing Jesus' talk of his coming arrest and death, maybe Peter was trying to prevent Jesus from being arrested for tax evasion. When Peter came to Jesus about the tax, Jesus answered before Peter asked. "What do you think, Simon? From whom do the kings of the earth collect customs or poll-tax, from their sons or from strangers?" (Matthew 17:25) Peter rightly answered taxes were collected from strangers to which Jesus responded, "Then the sons are exempt."

The implication is Jesus is the Son of God and exempt from these human taxes on a divine institution. Jesus already laid out the ultimate price he was going to pay just three verses earlier, much more than any tax. But Jesus told Peter to throw a hook into the sea and the first fish he caught would have the money for the tax in its mouth. It was with this Peter was to pay the tax collector (Matthew 17:27). Often people interpret this passage as a miracle. Jesus caused a fish to bite Peter's hook and it had money in its mouth. But I believe there was no fish at all. I believe Jesus was being sarcastic. Certainly, Jesus could have performed such a miracle, but conspicuously missing from the text is narrative stating Peter actually went fishing. So often when Scripture narratives state a command, a description of the command being carried out usually follows. We never read of Peter actually catching the aquatic wallet and paying the tax. Maybe this demonstrates Jesus was capable of righteous sarcasm, something I too often attempt to mimic and unsuccessfully so, the righteous part that is! I have the sarcasm down pat.

All of this brought confusion to the disciples. They saw Jesus glorified on a mountaintop. He cast out demons when their faith failed. He predicted his arrest and death. From mountaintop experiences to talk of death, it all made the disciples wonder where things stood. Is Jesus who he claims to be? But they saw his powers and the miraculous signs. Surely nothing could stop God's kingdom from taking over; it was simply a matter of when Jesus was going to pull the trigger. Maybe when Jesus debunked the religious establishment's taxes, the disciples saw it as an indicator Jesus was about to act. Thus, they wanted to know where they stood in the new regime. "Who then is the greatest in the kingdom of heaven?"

## BE CHILD-LIKE, NOT CHILDISH

Jesus answered by calling a child to come to him and said, "Truly I say to you, unless you are converted and become like children, you will not enter the kingdom of heaven. Whoever humbles himself as this child, he is the greatest in the kingdom of heaven." (Matthew 18:3-4) Unfortunately, we can read our modern, western ideal of children into this passage and miss the point. Jesus is not saying we are to become childish and naïve. He is not saying our faith is to be uninformed, simplistic, and free of questions. In the time and culture Jesus walked, children were second or even third class citizens. They were not the example to follow, but were to follow the example of men. Jesus is not giving his disciples a greeting-card cliché about faith, but a radical command. To become like a child in their culture was to debase oneself. It meant giving up any claim to rights or privileges. In order for someone to become great in the kingdom of heaven, they must give up their life! This was as counter to the disciples' culture as it is for ours.

Jesus even declared those who cause people with this child-like faith (not childish faith) to stumble would face terrible judgment. Jesus promised the wrongs would be brought to justice. It is on that note, Jesus went on to repeat a teaching he shared in the Sermon on the Mount (Matthew 5). He employed the metaphor of cutting off the hand that causes us to sin and throwing it away. Once again, we are to radically purge evil from our lives. We are to be holy. When we fail to be holy, we cause others of faith to stumble and suffer. Our choices impact others and our hypocrisy must be cut off and thrown away. Jesus is not calling us to skip through the flowery countryside of comfortable discipleship. He is calling us to take up our cross and die to self.

# BECOME AN ANCIENT CHILD

My son Jacob struggles with this just as much as any of us. Our culture does the exact opposite of the first-century Palestinian culture. Children in our culture are taught to be the center of the universe. Our children can become the priority over our marriage and even our relationship with God. Family schedules, finances and choices begin to center around the child. Couples put their marriage below the needs of their children. Certainly, a couple will have to make sacrifices for their children, but should never do so to the point the marriage falls by the wayside. It is in the best interest of the children for the marriage to not only survive, but thrive. We have tried our best to give this to our children. At times we fail, but our job is to prepare Jacob to become an adult. This means he will have to face pain, discomfort and disappointment. "As parents, we often want to protect our children from the world and that is a good thing. However, if we protect them from everything then they will not be prepared for anything."[xxx] Just as God told the sea, "Thus far you shall come, but no farther," (Job 38:11) we can allow an ap-propriate amount of pain into our children's lives at appropriate times. We can't teach our children the coping skills they will need as adults if we insulate them from everything difficult. We can teach them how to walk through pain, disappointment, and even pleasure with a Christ-like attitude. However, we can only give them what we possess ourselves.

I found another entry on Jacob's webpage from June 2008. This was the first time Macayla had a grand mal seizure:

> Jacob hurt his finger playing with a pocket door in our bathroom that we have told him not to play with multiple times. I had a headache all day and when Jacob hurt his finger, I was not the most compassionate father. I was short with him and not very understanding. In the midst of half-heartedly consoling him, Macayla's started having grand mal seizures. During those seizures, Macayla stopped breathing. She turned gray and her eyes glazed over. She was slipping away. In a panic, I yelled at Macayla to "breathe!" Jacob heard me and came in the room. He saw that I

had tears on my face and he asked what he could do to help. The only thing that came out of my mouth was, "Pray! Pray that Macayla will start breathing again." Jacob responded, "O.k." in a very matter-of-fact tone. He took two steps down the hall and prayed out loud. He said, "God can you help Macayla stop choking and start breathing again? Could you do it today, like right this instant?"

Within a few seconds of Jacob finishing that prayer, Macayla spit out a lot of mucus and began breathing again. Once Macayla seemed stable, I began to clean things up. Jacob came back to the room carrying a bottle of Diet Pepsi (my favorite soda) and said, "Dad I brought you something to make you feel better." I had to hug him and ask his forgiveness. I told him that when he hurt his finger, I had not been very nice. But when I was upset and scared he came along side and prayed and comforted me. I told him he was being a bigger man than I was. He hugged me and gently patted my back and said, "It's o.k. Dad." It is quite humbling to be Jacob's Dad.

Matthew 18 begins with Jesus telling us to become like a child and to purge evil from our lives. Is it not interesting the text immediately turns to relationships and forgiveness? Take the time to read Matthew's Gospel here and read it carefully. Jesus not only tells us to give up our lives, but to share the forgiveness we have received with others. When Jesus speaks of forgiveness, he is not speaking of an emotional release. When someone we know commits evil, he is not telling us to just let it roll off of us like water on a duck's back. We are to confront the issue head-on and with love. If someone sins against us, we aren't meant to quietly suppress our hurt and never let the other person know. If someone's sin is obvious and not necessarily against us, then we are to confront the issue in private and in love. If necessary, we may need to get others involved to help address the issue. Nowhere has Jesus spoken of forgiveness as simply an emotional, feel-good form of psychotherapy free of confrontation. There are times when confrontation may not be possible or even successful (see Matthew 18:17), but we can still forgive them as shown in verses 21-22. The overall message here is that we preserve relationships and practice forgiveness with action, not simply emotions. Jesus included two strong warnings in this discourse (see verses 18 and 35). How we handle our relationships and forgiveness has eternal ramifications. Christ gave all to forgive all and restore us to himself for eternity. Let our relationships reflect and pass on this amazing grace. When we become like a child and understand this metaphor in the ancient sense, others come first.

This boils down to holiness. Scripture in both the Old and New Testaments give us a list of rules and commands by which to live. But following rules is not the goal of holiness nor does outwardly following a set of rules make one holy. The rules should never be a substitute for holiness. These commands are practical ways to avoid sin and point us toward holiness. To avoid sin is to preserve our relationship with God and others. The rules must be followed both inwardly and outwardly. This is holiness; this is becoming like a child. It means we humble ourselves. We abandon our agenda and receive God's agenda in its place. As Zacharias stated, this is a miracle only the Master can perform. By the Master's grace, through faith we are given the power to change. The same grace that saves us transforms us. The same cross that atoned for our sins puts our agenda to death and opens us up to God's purpose each day of our sanctification. It is by Christ, the Light of the world, we can see the sin in our lives that needs removal. Jacob's webpage entry from April 2010 helps us here:

> At bedtime, Jacob told about the Bible lesson he learned at AWANA... Nicodemus came to Jesus in the night to ask him questions. Jacob's teachers used the night as a metaphor for the darkness of Nicodemus' heart but coming to Jesus brought light into Nicodemus' life. I asked Jacob if he understood what they meant about the darkness of his heart. He said he didn't. I said, "It's when you have thoughts or do things that you know are bad and you don't want mom, dad or anyone to see."

He objected, "I didn't do anything!"

I reassured him I was not accusing him of anything. I said, "Jacob we all have thoughts or do things we don't want others to know about."

"Even you?" he asked.

"Even me."

"Well, then all of us would have that everyday!" he said.

"That's right," I continued, "and that's why we need to go to Jesus everyday. Look at your room. Is it messy or clean?"

"Messy," he responded with annoyance.

"With the light on, we can see how messy it is. With the light off, we cannot tell. Think of your room as a metaphor for you heart and mind. Everyday you need to go to Jesus so he can turn on the light and show you the mess. Then he can help you clean it up!"

"Oh, I get it," he said.

"In fact," I continued, "you need to clean up your room each day! It will help you remember that it is a metaphor for your heart."

"Oh man!" he complained, "I hate metaphors!" There was a pause, and then he asked, "What is a metaphor?"

We may say we hate metaphors, but we really hate what they call us to do. We must let the Light shine into our lives and expose what needs to change. The fact remains: if we truly belong to Christ, we must actually change. This change does not occur simply through time and experience. As my friend, Gene Ownbey once said in a sermon, "We ascribe to evolution when it comes to discipleship. We seem to think we are just going to mature slowly over time." Being a Christian for forty years does not automatically indicate a person is a mature Christian. The assumption our maturity will simply come through the effects of time and sincerity is a way to avoid facing our flaws. Darwin claimed evolution happened in nature through mutations and natural selection. Many Christians seem to think their discipleship will happen this way but it only leads to a mutation of the Gospel and childish (not child-like) faith becomes the natural selection. Maturity comes when we surrender our agenda each day to Christ and take his agenda in its place. Maturity comes when we ask God to show us our flaws and sins so they can be remedied according to God's word. Maturity comes when we humble ourselves and become like a child. Maturity comes through holiness. It is the answer to our suffering. It is the answer to our prosperity. It is the answer to our grief. It even helps us with the question, "Why?"

### ONE…TWO…THREE…GO!

In the spring of 2007, three years before her death, Macayla was saying her last word. It was the word, "Go!" Macayla's occupational and physical therapists would put her on top of a short slide and count to three. If Macayla responded, "Go!" she could slide. She loved it and we still have video of her laughing with each slide. She was so motivated by the slide, she held on to that word even when all she could say was "Ghhhhhhh!" Macayla's last word was also what God wants us to do. We are to do more than simply ponder faith and God. We are called to action and action that is centered on truth and holiness. When we received the diagnosis, we were tempted to circle the wagons and ball up in tears. But we decided in the doctor's parking lot to live life. It was not the life we planned or anticipated for our family, but it was the life we had. Macayla needed to experience her life and her purpose just like the rest of us. Hiding and wallowing in self-pity was not what God wanted for us.

After Macayla died, we faced this same temptation of balling up and drowning in our grief and questions. But God's answer was the same. Jacob, Jennifer and I were called into action after Macayla died. We could not allow our grief to disrupt our relationship with God in disobedience driven by self-pity. Macayla's life had purpose and for us to rollover and do nothing dishonored that purpose. Our lives have purpose and to not live accordingly is to live apart from God. We certainly have healthy moments alone in our grief to shed tears as needed, but tears and grief cannot be allowed to define us. God's grace and God's strength can be shown in our weakness. The struggle for most of us is that we focus on our weakness and God's power is missed. We must step out of the way and let God's grace flow and it will engulf our weaknesses.

Jacob, Jennifer and I had to go. We knew we had to go back to where God called us before hurricanes and Battens disease. We were headed back to New Orleans. This was troubling for Jacob. He was only two the first time. He was seven when this plan resurfaced and he was concerned about leaving friends behind and the fact his dog would not be able to live on campus with us. But God says go and we cannot allow dogs, friends, houses or even family to prevent us from following him. This was a hard transition for Jacob and he did not wholeheartedly jump at the idea when it first came up. But Scripture never defines faith as merely an intellectual assent. Biblical faith involves action. Biblical faith involves real change, not simply chanting a creed or agreeing sincerely with the pastor's sermon. Biblical faith is always associated with going, doing and changing. For Jacob this meant the reality of giving up a dog to be where God wanted him. It meant being in a new place that was not as comfortable, though it was by no means horrible. It meant doing what his big sister told him to do: "GO!" This was Macayla's sermon that God used for Jacob and the rest of us.

Certainly, there are days for us that it is difficult to "GO!" We struggle with the gaping hole in our family. I stay busy and distracted but eventually the reality of her absence finds me, clenching my heart and mind. She is gone. She is supposed to be here, but her room is not hers. It is a guest room now. While it was still set up as hers, it hurt even more, for every time I walked in everything was in place except Macayla. There are moments I fear I will forget things about her. Will I remember her face? Will I forget what it was like to hold her? Not only do circumstances have a way of defining us outwardly, but at times we can allow the emotions and fears they create to define us inwardly as well. I have found others who have lost loved ones share these feelings. Memories bring emotions and help with the grieving process, but I must be careful. I must be careful to not allow those emotions and grief to consume. Grief must be a process and not a destination. In my grief, Jesus says, "Follow Me!" In my grief, Macayla's last word echoes, "GO!"

Jesus told the disciples to go. They were to take the boat out on the Sea of Galilee. Soon, Peter and the other disciples found themselves struggling to row their boat through rough seas. They were not cheerfully singing, "Row, row, row your boat gently down the stream…" Jesus came walking to them on the water, which frightened them even more than the wind and waves. Impulsive Peter, upon hearing Jesus identify himself, said, "Lord, if it is You, command me to come to You on the water." And He said, "Come!" Peter walked on water also. You would think this would be all it would take and Peter's faith would be unshakable, but in just moments, his faith shriveled as the waves and wind frightened him. Fear collapsed his faith. Life is not "but a dream" as the song goes, but presents real dangers and real blessings. How nice it would be if life was simply a gentle stream, and it is sometimes. But there are real storms to row through and it is easy to lose our paddles. It is easy to take our eyes off Christ and focus on the wind and waves. We can forget that Jesus told us to go out on that lake, knowing a storm was coming. In any circumstance, we must seek Christ and his perspective or we will drown. We must remember he has a purpose for sending us (See Matt. 14:22-33).

"GO!" We cannot let our "faith" be a slogan or cliché or it will drown in fear and circumstances. This word "faith" must encompass not only what our mind accepts as possible and our hearts are sincere about. It must reflect the knowledge of what is true, even if we cannot see it or touch it. Faith is a life lived according to that truth and this truth, which we cannot see or touch, clarifies the circumstances we can see and touch. "GO!" is not a command to be comfortable. "GO!" is not a command to have what we want when we want it. "GO!" means our faith has hands, feet and teeth. Tell a four-year-old child to go somewhere new and they will most likely run. Why do we stay frozen when God tells us to go somewhere new? If we run, it is often in the opposite direction. Going where God wants us may mean sacrifice from our perspective. It may mean Jacob loses a dog. But nothing we sacrifice compares to Christ's sacrifice on the cross. "GO!" means we no longer have to live with the sense that everything from church to bill collectors are competing for our time, money and resources. When we realize it all belongs to God, there is no competition! Our time, money, and energy are all his and to live a life on the "GO!" means living for him.

# THE NEW IDENTITY

This brings us all back to a crucial question as we face the path ahead. "Am I a child of God?" Before we can be a child of God, we must admit our sin has separated us from him forever and there is nothing in our own power that can undo this. One of the simplest definitions of sin I have ever heard was given during a Child Evangelism Fellowship workshop for Good News Clubs. They defined it as, "Anything you think, say or do that breaks God's heart or violates his word." Consider how your thoughts, words and actions match up to God's desires and his Word. This obviously means we have to know God's heart and his word. As stated earlier, when we see God clearer, we see ourselves with greater clarity. We see our situation with more clarity as well.

It states in 2 Corinthians 3:17-18 ESV, "Now the Lord is the Spirit, and where the Spirit of the Lord is, there is freedom. And we all, with unveiled face, beholding the glory of the Lord, are being transformed into the same image from one degree of glory to another. For this comes from the Lord who is the Spirit." Robert Mounce points out the two Greek participles in verse 18 that are keys to Christian transformation. The words translated as "beholding" and "being transformed" are present-tense participles. This tense in Greek participles means the action they describe is ongoing and continuous. As we continually behold God and His glory, we are continually transformed. As Mounce states it, "The transformation keeps pace with the contemplation. They are inextricably bound together. By continuing to behold the glory of the Lord we are continually being transformed into his image."[xxxi]

We may be tempted to think this suggests we simply sit around and contemplate God then go about our day as we usually would. However, the point is that the contemplation reshapes our thoughts and worldview and this changes our choices and responses in daily life. It means we see the truth and the truth makes us free, for where the Spirit of the Lord is, there is freedom. To be a child of God means we recognize and admit our sin and believe that the only remedy for it is found in Christ Jesus. His death on the cross paid the just wrath we deserve for our sin. His resurrection from the tomb declares victory over sin and death and is the reality of our new life in him. Then we simply ask him to be the Lord or our lives, not just the Savior. Through this, we become the adopted child of God the Father. We are fellow heirs of the kingdom with Christ. When we can truly call God "our Father," then we know our present sufferings in this smaller portion of reality do not compare to the glory that is to be revealed to us (Romans 8:14-18). Being a child of God is not simply about status, but is about the ultimate reality that is being fully revealed. It is about how we live here and now. It impacts how we live through prosperity and pain.

Jacob's page entry from December 2, 2010, Eternal Security...In Jesus the Good Ole Boy:

> The other night, Jacob was saying his prayers silently. When he was finished, he said he wondered if he really asked Jesus into his heart last year. I asked him what he thought and a shrug of the shoulders was the only answer.
>
> I was able to remind him of the story of his profession. For a couple of years we had been working on how to pray. I taught him to start off with praising God and think of things that are amazing about God. (All-powerful, all-knowing, the Trinity, etc.) Then he needed to confess anything he had done wrong and ask for forgiveness and help to not do it again. Then to thank God for all the blessings in his life and end with asking God to do things for him and others. For over a year and a half, when we would get to the confession portion of the prayer, Jacob would simply say he had not done anything wrong that day. I never pressed him here. I wanted him to come to this on his own.
>
> I reviewed this story with Jacob and assured him that he came to realize Christ's work in his heart over a period of time. Jacob began asking forgiveness on his own for sins he had previously ignored in his life. He began to put things together on his own by taking different teachings from the Bible and see how they are woven together to show us God's offer of grace and redemption. Jacob came to that place by God's grace and it was not forced upon him, nor manipulated. I reassured him that all

testimony of his journey points to the truth that Christ is living in him and working on him in amazing ways. I also assured him this would not be the last time he would question his faith.

Of course, the one Scripture that jumped into my mind for him was John 10:27-28. Here Jesus, the Good Shepherd is telling the crowds and us that His sheep (disciples) know Him and He knows them. In other words, we have a relationship with Him. He gives His sheep eternal life and "they shall never perish" and "no one can snatch them from His hand." Just the day before Jacob was questioning his faith, I had been studying an article about this text. In the Greek, when Jesus said, "they shall never perish," it uses something akin to a double negative. Transliterated, it reads, "they not never perish." This is poor English, but proper Koine Greek allows it and uses it in this case to emphasize that there is no way possible for His sheep to perish (i.e. go to Hell).[xxxii]

I shared this with Jacob and told him about the double negative. I said, "We hear it used in the South by some people, such as, 'I ain't got no...'" Jacob said, "Or, I don't got no..." I told him that Jesus said we will not perish so strongly and meant it so much that when John translated His words into Greek, he had to use a double negative. It may also mean that Jesus was a country boy and the South is indeed God's country! Jacob thought that was funny, and he seemed to rest a little better.

But for those of us who struggle to know if our baptism or profession of faith was real, I say God can help us know for sure. Often, adults who were baptized as a child look back and say that they did not or could not understand what they were doing. I would advise caution there. Certainly, a child may make a profession to please a parent or adult in their life, but the reality is that we do not fully understand baptism or all the realities at play during our profession of faith, irrespective of age.

We can know that we need a Savior. But there is still a mystery at work in our baptism and profession of faith. God's sovereignty is weaving our choices into His plan. He is inwardly drawing us to Him and yet wants us to outwardly express that drawing through baptism. All this to say, just because we may not fully understand the dynamics of our baptism, God does. He doesn't mess it up!

In Genesis, Jacob and Esau traded their identity. Esau traded who he was for a bowl of stew. Jacob traded his soul for the pocket-change of an earthly inheritance. However, God did not leave Jacob to be Jacob. God challenged Jacob and gave him a new identity as Israel. Christ wants to give us a new identity as well. Jesus said we are to come to him as a child and we get confused as to what this means and what it looks like. Ancient children were not acknowledged in public. They were not the center of the universe. They were third-class citizens. How astonishing to realize Jesus came to us as a child in a time when children were not as esteemed! He was not a result of Mary and Joseph's union. Joseph had no obligation to be Jesus' earthly father, but being a righteous man and open to God, Joseph adopted Jesus as his own. This he did in spite of the risk and fallout of marrying a woman who all assumed was an adulteress. Joseph's adoption of Jesus gave Jesus an identity as a son of David and this was a necessary part of God's plan for the Messiah. Jesus had to be adopted by an earthly father so we could be adopted by the heavenly Father. Christ, in the days of his flesh, was from the family line of Judah and the priestly line of Melchizedek (see Hebrews 5-10). His adoption in earthly terms led to our adoption in eternal terms. Our Creator endured an earthly identity, which put him on a cross so that we who believe could have a heavenly identity. We no longer have to be defined by our sin, circumstances, successes or failures. When we become a child of God, our identity is no longer subject to the whims of situations, but is set for eternity. This not only changes how we will live after death, but how we live today. Who is the greatest in the kingdom of Heaven? Those who become an ancient child.

## SELF-ASSESSMENT

1. Are you a child of God? Why or why not? If so, do you understand it enough that you could explain it to a child?
2. Have you tried to circumvent or avoid the path and relationships God has for you?
3. What are you doing to help develop your spiritual maturity?
4. When you pray, is it just for God to address the circumstances of your life or do you ever pray for him to show you what needs to change in your character?
5. Would you describe your faith as something more internal and private or active and impacting those around you? (Certainly, faith is personal, but true faith cannot be private!)

If you do not have a Bible study plan or routine in place, start by spending just ten minutes in it each day this week. Stay on the same verses or at least in the same book until you pull as much out as possible. Pray for God to illuminate your heart and mind to see what the text says, what it does NOT say, and what it reveals about God first. How does the text point to Christ and what He did? Then seek what changes need to happen in your heart and character because of this truth. Next, change, go and do!

# 11

# New Hope

*The Story of Our Grief*

The rock bench I was sitting upon was cold and that is to be expected in the mountains of western North Carolina on a November morning. Down the hill from me, the New River quietly slipped by and the honking geese were happy to drift on its current. The sun was cresting over the mountaintop behind me and burning off the remaining fog in the valley. I was sitting in the beginning stage of a garden on the side of a mountain overlooking the river at Camp New Hope. This was the forth year we had come to this retreat, but the first year without Macayla. The bench I was sitting upon had Macayla's name engraved on it with butterflies and the sentence, "In Christ, nothing separates us from God's love." Macayla loved this place. She was an outdoors girl and we had so many great memories of her rolling around in the grass, laughing as she sat in the cold, river water and riding on the bumpy mountain trails with joy on every bounce. But this morning, I was struggling to find joy. I want my life back. I want Macayla back and I would take her any way I could get her, disabled or not. I said, "God, You had better be real! You better be who You say You are. I want to see my little girl again! There better be a heaven!"

Camp New Hope was started by two brothers, Mark and Will Adkins, for the sole purpose of hosting children with life-threatening medical conditions and their families for a week of vacation at no charge. Macayla loved coming to this place. It was one of the few places where we could truly relax and Macayla enjoy being there as much as she enjoyed being home. The Adkins only came in for visits, but left the camp and its daily activities in the capable hands of Randy Brown and her band of volunteers. But on one of our stays, Will Adkins came for a visit and brought his dog, Swiper. We thought this was a great name because Macayla loved the fox, Swiper, from *Dora the Explorer*. During that visit, I sat on the floor with Macayla and Swiper came over and began licking her on the face. She exploded into laughter and giggles and she continued laughing the rest of that afternoon. She loved dogs. We love that memory.

But these memories can be hard and sitting on this same mountain without her was hard. Jennifer, Jacob and I each struggle with grief uniquely. Each of us finds comfort in different things at different times and in different ways, and as tempting as it is, we cannot force others to grieve our way. Jacob goes through cycles of unexplained anger followed by emotional ups and downs that can change minute by minute. It will continue sometimes for a couple of days and end with a burst of tears at bedtime. He gets this pattern from his father as I experience a similar cycle. Jennifer stays busy and crashes when the reality of grief catches up with her. She even expresses surprise over what affects her and what does not. She was ready to change Macayla's room into a guest room about two months after Macayla left, but a box of photographs of Macayla sat on our bedroom floor for over six months as she would occasionally peruse them but never put them up. As we continued our walk through grief, two entries from our blog came about during this time:

The Continuous Love of God in Pain, blog for October 26, 2010:

> You can have a mixture of comfort and fear if you read the eleventh chapter of John's Gospel. It is the story where Mary and Martha's brother, Lazarus, became ill. They sent word to Jesus who was at a distance. This story can stir up fear because upon hearing the news, Jesus did not come to Lazarus. He did not heal him. He *purposefully* waited for two days after receiving the news before taking action. As a result, Lazarus died from his illness. We don't like a God who would do that. We want a God who will jump into action and save the day!

Upon hearing the report of Lazarus' illness, Jesus responded, "This sickness is not to end in death, but for the glory of God, so that the Son of God may be glorified by it." Yet, as we read on, Lazarus died. Now, for those familiar with the story, we know that Jesus showed up after Lazarus had been buried and Jesus raised him from the dead. That's amazing, of course, but experience tells us that Jesus does not perform this miracle very often. It is even a rare occurrence in the Bible. So, this makes us uneasy about God. He is not a tame God. We cannot compel Him to do things our way and in our time of need, that makes it hard to know from where our comfort will come. Jesus said this illness would be for the glory of God and for His glory. But if we are honest, we just want our loved one healed. We are less interested in honoring God. We just want Jesus to save the day...right now...in our way.

But John includes something interesting in the original language. Right after Jesus declares this will result in God's glory, John wrote, "Now Jesus loved Martha and her sister and Lazarus. So, when He heard that he [Lazarus] was sick, He then stayed two days longer in that place where He was." (John 11:5-6) John did not have to include the line, "Now Jesus loved Martha and her sister and Lazarus." He could have just reported that Jesus remained where he was for two days. But there is something important in this line and it does not come through in our English translations with the literary strength intended by the Greek.

In English, we are interested in when the action of a verb takes place; past, present or future. As in "I loved" or "I love" or "I will love." But the Greeks were more interested in the kind of action. Their verbs tell us if the action was ongoing and this was important to them. It needs to be important for us in this verse. When John wrote, "Now Jesus loved Martha and her sister and Lazarus," he could have used a form of the verb that would translate just "loved." But John used a tense in Greek that is reserved for continuous action. The form of the word love could be translated, "Jesus was loving" or "was continuing to love" Martha and her sister and Lazarus. *So*, when He heard that he was sick, He then stayed two days longer in the place where He was.

This small difference gives us a better feel for the emphasis John is giving. Jesus was loving Martha, Mary and Lazarus in the midst of His seeming non-response. Jesus knew the full outcome of the situation. He knows it for ours as well. He even knows it for the people He does not raise from the tomb like Lazarus. He knows it for those He heals or does not heal. He knows the full outcome for those left behind as well. When pain and loss come, we often look to Christ as Mary and Martha did and say, "Lord, if You had been here...if you had just stepped in and intervened, then this would not have happened." Certainly, He knows this. But He knows better than any of us where the true miracle lies in our situation. He could simply fix it and sometimes He does. But maybe the greater miracle is we walking through our situation in a way that glorifies Him and leads others to Him. Maybe the greatest miracle is the change our situation will bring to our lives and the lives of others. Jesus "was loving" Martha, Mary and Lazarus through His delay. Is He not doing the same for His other disciples? His love is continuous and His response to His disciples' struggles, whatever that response is, will always be in that love.

Macayla's Soundtrack, blog for November 15, 2010:

Shortly after Mac went home, I compiled some songs to use in some home videos. These songs were meaningful to us and to Macayla. The

CD is in Jennifer's car, which I happen to be driving today. I listened to it.

The "Bare Necessities" from Disney's *Jungle Book* was on there as was "Hakuna Matata" from *The Lion King*. Macayla loved those movies and those songs. Even after she was immobile, I would help her dance to these songs by moving her hands to the rhythm (which was not too good considering I have no rhythm!) But she would smile so big. I miss dancing with my girl.

Another song on there is "Held" by Natalie Grant. It is from her 2005 *Awaken* CD. The lyrics to this song are about situations like ours and what it means for believers. One line always jumps out at me:

> If hope is born of suffering;
>
> If this is only the beginning,
>
> Can we not wait for one hour
>
> Watching for our Savior?

It always brings the picture to mind of Jesus in the Garden of Gethsemane asking His disciples to keep watch while He prayed. They kept falling asleep while Jesus agonized over what was coming. He asked them, "So, you men could not keep watch with Me for one hour? Keep watching and praying that you may not enter into temptation; the spirit is willing but the flesh is weak." (Mt. 26:40-41) They kept falling asleep as Jesus grieved over what was to come. The hope of salvation was about to be born in Christ's suffering and they slept. Jesus' prayer was the beginning of His suffering for our sin. It was the beginning of the Easter story that brings eternal life to those who believe and confess Christ as their Lord. But the disciples slept.

Certainly, Macayla's death was the beginning of eternity for her. Our lives on earth are but blips on a screen compared to the eternity we will face. Christ was very clear on this point. We either face an eternity with Him or an eternity separated from Him. His blood spilt on the cross atones for our sins, the sins that separate us from God. The suffering on the cross was a literal Hell on earth, yet so many of us let this reality slip past us as if we are asleep. Jesus' death and resurrection offers forgiveness and restoration, yet we sleep through this truth as well. We do not have to wait until our deathbed to experience the eternity we are headed for. With Christ we can get tastes of heaven on earth, a preview of the glory that is to come, yet we sleep through this too. All too often I am so wrapped up in my circumstances that I sleep through the greater reality and truth of Christ.

Macayla's soundtrack reminded me to stay awake and pray. Keep watch for what my Savior is doing in my life and what He is calling me to do. It is bittersweet to listen to her music and remember her smiles and dancing. It is hard to say "Hakuna Matata" or "It Is Well with My Soul." But Macayla and her life had the "Fingerprints of God" all over them as she lived a "Life Less Ordinary." On hard days, I have to remember that God "Led Me" and so "I Will Praise [Him] in this Storm." When my blip of a life is over and I enter eternity, Macayla will be there. We will see the abundant life Christ gave us, far beyond just the "Bare Necessities!" We will see that in our worst suffering on earth, we were indeed "Held" by nail-scared hands.

In trust and faith by grace, we can wait on our Lord. I sat in a garden of stone and flowers near the base of a mountain overlooking a river valley. This peaceful setting was juxtaposed by my anguish over having to wait to see my girl again; my anguish was about loss and separation. Like Mary and Martha, I had called for my Lord to save the day, but he did not come when I wanted. Jesus also sat in a garden, a garden of olive trees at the base of a mountain overlooking a river valley. This peaceful setting of Gethsemane's garden was juxtaposed with his anguish over the coming pain and wrath he would soon face; anguish over loss and separation. His human will anguished to follow the divine will. My garden anguish cannot compare to his. He endured that anguish for the joy set before him, the joy of reconciling the children with the Father. Because he endured that anguish, this father has the joy set before him, as I will be reunited with both my daughter and my Father. Can I not wait for one hour, watching for my Savior?

We must let truth eclipse grief, success and failure. Truth points us to God and God is holy. "You shall be holy, for I am holy." Holiness redefines us and gives us not only the launching point from which to face our circumstances, but the grounding and strength to walk through them. By God's grace, he offers this holiness as a gift through Jesus Christ. Let us receive it and be a child of God. Truth points us to an eternal and sovereign God, working all things together for the good of those who love him and are called according to his purpose. This eternity does not mean our current circumstances are unimportant; quite the contrary. Our circumstances will be part of the eternal plan and must be kept in the proper perspective. We must let go of our agenda and "perfect plans" and grab on to the plan of God. Those who lose their life for the Gospel and Christ's sake will gain life, even in the valley of the shadow of death.

# Acknowledgements

WE ARE INDEBTED to the faithful prayers and love of so many who walked this journey with us. Our parents and siblings supported us financially, prayerfully, and most of all by their presence. Nana came often, cleaned the house, fed us and spoiled Jacob. BB & Papa made date nights possible, mixed meds and kept the DVD's playing. They filled in for us more times than can be remembered and spoiled Jacob. Grammy and Pappy brought wheelchair ramps, fun times and Outback even when it meant late-night drives back home. And, they spoiled Jacob. Macayla's grandparents made her time here so much better. Thanks for spoiling her, us and Jacob! Thank you to my sister, Austin, for putting up with random manuscripts and poor writing. Thanks to Harrison and the nieces for an afternoon in Whoville! Thanks to all our family for being there, even at the end. I know it was hard to watch.

We are grateful to our Bible Fellowship Group at Edwards Road Baptist Church in Greenville, SC. They did not let the 45 minute drive deter them from loving on our family on a regular basis. To the prayer warriors at both Edwards Road Baptist and Electric City Fellowship, thank you. Your faithful prayers filled the gap more than you can know. You not only prayed for us but also filled our pantry and bellies on many occasions. God has blessed us with many great cooks! Thanks to Richard and Susan for making us a part of their family of faith in Anderson. Thanks to David and Anne and the folks of Oakwood Baptist for loving on us and teaching our son so much. Thank you to Locust Hill Baptist in Travelers Rest, SC for the support, love in cards and sliced cheese! Thank you Fred at Aiken FBC and to all the siblings in Christ scattered everywhere who put us on your prayer lists and lifted us up to the Father.

Thanks to Gene & Angie Ownbey for walking with us and helping us walk her down the aisle. To Charlie Summey for the much needed laughter, advice, accountability and being my friend and brother. Thank you to Larry & Debbie Sherman for making smoaksignal.com possible. God has used this in ways we never saw coming. Thanks to Michelle, Jeff, Michael and Daniel Johnson for the advice, support and great meals together. Thanks to John &

Shelley McGuirt for continuing to support us, mentor us and for leading the team of hardwood floor installers! I pray, John, this work contributes to the treasure being laid up in heaven. Thank you to our great neighbors, David, Linda, Wayne and Cynthia, who prayed, mowed our lawn without asking, and kept an eye on things for us. Thanks to Tina and Richard for sharing your boys with Jacob. We are so grateful to the wonderful teachers Macayla and Jacob have had during this time in Anderson District Five. Miss Judy kept us straight and introduced Macayla to her "boyfriend," Hunter. Now we are friends with the rest of Hunter's family and blessed by their support. Thanks to Miss Patty & Miss Elaine, Ms. Patterson, Ms. Moss, and Ms. Roper for helping Jacob through.

Special thanks go to Pediatric Therapy Works and the great work they do. Sharon, Cecile, Cathy, the late Joy and others taught us so much. We are most grateful for your prayers and the smiles you gave our girl! Thanks to Dr. Morales and Cathy for giving us your cell phone number and answering our questions. Thanks for thinking outside the box and doing what it took to make your girl more comfortable. Thanks to Dr. Tracey for being more than a pediatrician, but a friend. You made things happen when they needed to. Thanks to Dr. Gretchen for going above and beyond those last few days with Macayla and continuing to check on us. Thanks, Michael, for doing so much more than just running the EEG. Dr. Curtis Rogers and Brooke made genetics not only enjoyable but also spiritual. Thanks for your love, prayers and spending so much time with us. Thanks to the pediatric floor of the Greenville Hospital System and great nurses like Marissa. We are thankful to Dr. Chandler and Kim for the feeding tube we never wanted but were glad we had. Janet and the crew in Pediatric GI kept Macayla growing. Thanks for the backaches! Dr. Tony helped us understand Macayla's vision and gave us hope when we weren't sure if she could see us. Steve at Equipped for Life worked miracles to get Mac her stuff and her food. Thank you.

Thank you Mr. Gene for being there so faithfully the last year and for traveling with us on vacation. Thank you, Miss Donna for giving Macayla "spa days" and Hannah for being a great sister in Christ and nurse. Sonya Justice did an awesome job coordinating Pediatric Services of America's care of Macayla at home. We had some real angels show up those last days like Amanda and Dee who was the right person in the right place at the right time. Thanks, also, to the Make-A-Wish foundation for a great trip to Disney World. Thank you to Miss Randy at Camp New Hope. Your dedication and love helped us and so many others taste heaven on earth! We were so blessed by Family Connection and the hard work of Michelle and Sherry. We appreciate the assistance of the Battens Disease Support and Research Association for their ability to connect us with others in this journey. Hospice of the Upstate went above and beyond to guide us before, during and after Macayla's home-going. McDougald Funeral Home made some of our most daunting decisions more peaceful. We are so thankful for their gentleness and anticipating our needs.

There are so many who have faithfully read the blog and prayed for us. Some close and some from great distances. Thank you and I pray you will find God's blessing in new and abundant ways. Janice, Amy & Mark, Beth, Linda, Rich & Laurie, Angie & Gene, Paige, Michelle, Mike & Judy, Cathy B., Cathy S., Leslie and Hobbi, Janet, Carolyn, Traci, Doris, Anonymous, and so many others who peeked in for a visit. I wish I could mention everyone who has prayed, supported and been with us on this journey, but that would be another book itself. God's presence and strength is manifested through you all.

Most of all, we are thankful for the grace, strength and hope our Lord Jesus Christ has provided. Thank you for holding our girl and us in Your nail-scarred hands! We can't wait to see You and her again. "To live is Christ, to die is gain."

## Notes

i. Russell D. Moore, *Adopted for Life: The Priority of Adoption for Christian Families and Chruches*, (Crossway Books, Wheaton, IL, 2009) pg. 18.

ii. Actually, Jonah knew God would allow the Ninevites to repent as he indicates in his lament in chapter 4. He was hoping God would not show such mercy or that the Ninevites would not repent. Therefore, Jonah's message was ultimately a message of hope and had God's intended impact.

iii. David Platt, *Radical: Taking Back Your Faith from the American Dream* (Multnomah Books, Colorado Springs, CO, 2010) pg. 71

iv. Peter Kreft, "Why Debate the Existence of God?" in *Does God Exist? The Debate Between Theists and Atheists*, ed. William D. Watkins, J.P. Moreland & Kai Nielsen (Amherst, NY: Prometheus Books, 1993) pg. 23-24.

v. C.S. Lewis, "Right and Wrong as a Clue to the Meaning of the Universe," Book I, *Mere Christianity* (Touchstone, New York, 1996 edition).

vi. Neil Lightfoot, *How We Got The Bible*, (Baker Books, Grand Rapids, Mich. 2003) This is a great resource for anyone who wishes to learn more about how the Bible came to us in its present form. It is written for the general public and is not bogged down in scholarly debate. It gives a concise and clear picture. However, for those wishing to go deeper, consider Comfort, Philip, ed. & others, *The Origin of the Bible*, Tyndale Publishers, 2003.

vii. Gypsy Smith, quoted by Ravi Zacharias in *Is Your Church Ready?* ed. Ravi Zacharias and Norman Geisler (Zondervan Grand Rapids, Mich. 2003) pg. 22

viii. There is evidence to suggest that Tamar went to her half-brother, Amnon, to minister to him in a spiritual ceremony involving bread. Amnon was lusting after Tamar and feigned illness as a way to get David to send Tamar to him and make bread in front of him. There was a practice in the ancient Middle East among royalty that a woman would attend to the sick person and make a special meal and drink in a ceremony with the hopes of divine intervention and healing. See "Was habbirya a Healing Ritual Performed by a Woman in King David's House?" by Adrien Janis Bledstein, *Biblical Research* vol. 37, 1992 pg 15-31 Chicago Society of Biblical Research. The writer of Samuel could have omitted the details of how the rape occurred. The writer may have included these details in part to highlight the Deuteronomic curses coming to fruition.

ix. C.S. Lewis, *A Grief Observed* (Batam Books New York 1976) pg. 1-4.

x. Rev. William M. Taylor, *David, King of Israel: His Life and Its Lessons* (Harper & Brothers Publishers, New York, 1874) pg 291-298

xi. *The X-Files*, by Chris Carter, Fox Television 1993-2002

xii. Ravi Zacharias, *Recapture the Wonder* (Integrity Publishers, Nashville, TN, 2003) pg. 96.

xiii. Max Rogland, "The Covenant in the Book of Job," *Criswell Theological Review*, vol. 7, no. 1, Fall 2009, pg. 49-62. Rogland demonstrates the covenant nature of Job and God's relationship and his conclusions are what most who have suffered loss can attest. They feel as if God has betrayed them. We do not have to be under Deuteronomy's covenant to feel as if God has betrayed us. The language of Job carries the sense of a legal proceeding and there is a need to determine if God violated his covenant with Job, or as his friends assert, did Job violate his side of the bargain. When we suffer, has God violated us? What "covenant" do we have with Him?

xiv. Ravi Zacharias, *Beyond Opinion: Living the Faith We Defend*, Thomas Nelson, Nashville, TN 2007) pg. xviii.

xv. I am indebted to Dr. George Schwab for the concept of God "weaving" our choices into His sovereign plan. I believe it to be one of the best ways to describe what the Bible keeps in tension. The idea is not that our choices are some random force outside of God's plan that are brought in and mixed with it. The concept is that our choices are made and are real. We are responsible for them. However, they never determine God's plan. Instead, God "weaves" them into the proper place of His plan through His omniscience and infinite power.

xvi. Each of the plagues in Exodus demonstrates the frailty of an Egyptian god or the cult. First, the Nile turned to blood showed the utter weakness of the river god Hapi, also considered a giver of life for Egypt. Second, the plague of frogs was against Heget, a goddess who looked like a frog. The third plague of dust being turned into gnats was aimed at Egypt's priests. Flies of the fourth plague put Uatchit under God's control. The fifth plague against Egypt's cattle was a blow to Ptah, Hathor and other bovine deities. The cow was considered sacred. Sixth, the boils proved the healing deities such as Sekhmet worthless. The sky goddess, Nut, was shut out by the hailstorm in the seventh plague. Eighth, Isis and Seth could not protect the crops from the locusts. Ninth, Ra the sun god, was struck during the darkness. Finally, the Pharaoh slaughtered the firstborn of the Hebrews when Moses was born. The tenth plague struck Pharaoh and the gods of childbirth when the firstborn of Egypt was struck. For more, see *Old Testament Survey, The Message, Form, and Background of the Old Testament* by LaSor, Hubbard & Bush, Wm. B. Eerdman's Publishing Company, Grand Rapids, MI, 1996.

xvii. Calvin Miller, *Once Upon A Tree* (Howard Publishing, West Monroe, LA, 2002) pg. 49

xviii Matthew Lynch, "Bursting at the Seams: Phonetic Rhetoric in the Speeches of Elihu", *Journal of the Study of the Old Testament*, vol. 30 no. 3, 2006, pg. 345-364.

xix William B. Ward, *Out of the Whirlwind: A Study of the Book of Job* (John Knox Press Richmond, VA, 1958) pg. 101.

xx Ibid. pg. 104

xxi. George M. Schwab, "The Book of Job and Counsel in the Whirlwind", *The Journal of Biblical Counseling*, vol. 17, no. 1, Fall 1998, pg. 37-39.

xxii. Ibid., pg. 40-43

xxiii. Lewis, *A Grief Observed*, pg. 4-5

xxiv. Anselm, *Cur Deus Homo*, Joseph M. Colleran translator, Albany, New York: Magi Books, 1969. 2.7

xxv. Steven Curtis Chapman, "With Hope" from *Speechless*, June 15, 1999, Sparrow Label Group, Brentwood, TN.

xxvi. John Ortberg, *The Life You've Always Wanted* (Zondervan, Grand Rapids, Mich., 2002) pg. 36.

xxvii. Dennis Lindsey and Sean Kelly, "Issues in Small-Town Policing" in *The FBI Law Enforcement Bulletin*, July 2004, Vol. 73, no. 7, retrieved from on October 3, 2010 www.fbi.gov/publications/leb/2004/july2004/july04leb.htm#page_2

xxviii. Kenneth Scott Latourette, *A History of Christianity: Volume 1: to A.D. 1500* (Harper San Francisco, 1975) pg. 81-82.

xxix. Ravi Zacharias, *Recapture the Wonder* (Integrity Publishers, Nashville, TN, 2003) pg. xiii.

xxx. Jeff Smoak, "Protect or Prepare," in *ParentLife*, June 2010, pg. 28-29.

xxxi. Robert Mounce in *Basics of Biblical Greek Grammar* by William D. Mounce (Zondervan, Grand Rapids, MI, 2009) pg. 244.

xxxii. Buist M. Fanning, ibid. pg. 287.